THE BRUINS
IN BLACK AND WHITE
1924–1966

EDDIE SHORE. Eddie Shore was both the Babe Ruth and Ty Cobb of hockey—namely, a charismatic superstar who played with unmatched ferocity. Not only did Shore elevate the Bruins to championship status, but he also helped elevate the National Hockey League (NHL) to major-league status in the United States. His dynamic presence filled arenas across North America, and during his tenure, the "Original Six" was more accurately described as the "Original Ten" or "Original Twelve," with teams in St Louis, Pittsburgh, Philadelphia, and Brooklyn joining a league already populated with teams from Montreal (two), Toronto, Ottawa, Chicago, New York City, and Detroit. (Collection of the Sports Museum.)

THE BRUINS
IN BLACK AND WHITE
1924–1966

Richard A. Johnson and Brian Codagnone

ARCADIA
PUBLISHING

Published by Arcadia Publishing
Charleston, South Carolina

Library of Congress Catalog Card Number: 2003112716

For all general information contact Arcadia Publishing at:
Telephone 843-853-2070
Fax 843-853-0044
E-mail sales@arcadiapublishing.com
For customer service and orders:
Toll-Free 1-888-313-2665

Visit us on the Internet at www.arcadiapublishing.com

*This book is dedicated to Milton Conrad Schmidt and Woody Dumart,
as well as to all the men who proudly wore the colors of the Boston Bruins.*

COONEY WEILAND AND ART ROSS IN THE BRUINS LOCKER ROOM, C. 1937. Bruins coach and general manager Art Ross celebrates the Bruins consecutive victories to start the 1937–1938 season with star center Ralph "Cooney" Weiland and Ross's dog. In two seasons, Ross selected Weiland as his successor as the Bruins coach, and the former scoring ace led the team to a combined record of 58-20-18 with a Stanley Cup in his second and final year as coach in 1941. (Collection of the Sports Museum.)

CONTENTS

ACKNOWLEDGMENTS

This project would have been impossible were it not for the yeoman effort of my coauthor Brian Codagnone. He personifies the selfless code of old-time hockey and has been my winger on the Sports Museum line for many seasons. His knowledge of and enthusiasm for his beloved Bruins are evident on every page. We both undertook this project as a labor of love and have donated 100 percent of our royalties to the Sports Museum at Boston's Fleet Center, where we comprise the curatorial and facilities staff. The photographs and captions in this book are also the basis of an upcoming display within the museum.

We are grateful to Arcadia Publishing and Tiffany Howe (associate publisher) and former Arcadian Amy Sutton for their support of our efforts.

We are also grateful to the Sports Museum staff, including Michelle Gormley, Malcolm Graham (chairman), and Bill Galatis (former executive director).

The Sports Museum would not exist at the Fleet Center were it not for the generous and thoughtful support of Richard Krezwick, Harry Sinden, Jim Bednarek, John Wentzel, David Splaine, Mary Clivio, and the Jacobs family.

This book would not exist were it not for the collections made available to the museum from Milt Schmidt, the family of Walter Brown, George Owen, Mrs. Ralph Weiland, Woody Dumart, John Cronin and Al Thiebeault of the *Boston Herald*, Leslie Jones, Tina Anderson, J. Harvey McKenney, George Sullivan, Al Ruelle, Sinclair Hitchings, Aaron Schmidt, and the late Gordon Katz.

INTRODUCTION

In the beginning, the Boston Bruins were a rough tribe of Canadian tradesmen—athletic gypsies seeking their fortune with the first American franchise in the fledgling National Hockey League (NHL). At the time the Bruins played their first game, on December 1, 1924, the game of hockey was already a staple of the Boston sports scene. Teams from local preparatory schools and colleges formed the base of the first generation of American players. Stars such as Hobey Baker, George Owen, and Myles Lane dazzled capacity crowds at the Boston Arena while playing for Princeton, Harvard, and Dartmouth, respectively. Boston was also home to the first interscholastic hockey league in the country. The NHL could not have selected a better city in America in which to establish a franchise.

If the sporting heart of Greater Boston could be seen, it would resemble a hockey puck. The logo on that puck is, of course, the unmistakable black-spoked "B" of the Boston Bruins. Of all the professional sports franchises to play in Boston, none has sold a greater percentage of their tickets or performed before a more loyal contingent of fans. For decades, the figure of 13,909, representing the attendance total of a hockey sellout at the Boston Garden, was a constant fixture of all Bruin line scores at home.

Boston embraces the Bruins through good times and bad, in part because the city and surrounding suburbs are one of the great hotbeds of the game. In the 1920s and 1930s, the Bruins attracted the best local talent and showcased them on their feeder teams of the Bruin Cubs and Boston Olympics before giving them a chance in the NHL. Players such as the aforementioned George Owen of Newton and Myles Lane of Melrose, as well as Hago Harrington of Stoneham and Eddie Jeremiah of Worcester, were among the first Americans to serve their apprenticeship under Art Ross and skate in the big time with their mostly Canadian teammates. The fledgling franchise created fans and players in equal measure.

In only two generations, the multitude of young players inspired by the Bruins not only helped to beat the Russians twice but then went on to fill the rosters of collegiate and professional teams across North America. These players, in turn, have laced the blades on their sons and daughters, and so the game thrives. Everyone in the Boston area knows someone who has reached either the collegiate or professional level in the game. This is certainly not true with any other major sport. The Bruins symbolize both the deep roots of the game as well as the continuing hockey boom in the United States and remain the team that is closest to the hearts of the fans in America's greatest sports region.

For nearly 80 seasons, the Boston Bruins have served as the NHL's flagship franchise in the

United States. Not only were they the first NHL team in the continental United States, but they have also enjoyed as storied and colorful a history as any franchise in the history of North American professional sports. They are a team whose roster has included the likes of the mercurial Eddie Shore, a virtual Ty Cobb on skates; Aubrey V. "Dit" Clapper, a hockey "Iron Man" in the mold of Lou Gehrig who played both forward and defense with equal skill; the "Kraut Line" of Milton Conrad Schmidt, Woody Dumart, and Bobby Bauer; as well as the greatest player of all time, the incomparable No. 4, Bobby Orr. No less than 43 members of the Bruins are enshrined in the Hockey Hall of Fame. The Bruins five Stanley Cup championships are second only to the nine won by the Detroit Red Wings for teams based in the United States.

To recognize the significance of the Boston Bruins one must imagine the time in which they were founded. The national sports landscape was dominated by only one truly professional sport, major league baseball, with boxing a distant second. In baseball, Bostonians rooted for teams in both the American and National Leagues as well as countless local school and town teams. In amateur circles, Harvard's football team was the Rose Bowl champion in 1920 and regularly played before crowds of 60,000 at Harvard Stadium. At this time, the National Football League and National Basketball Association would have been almost unimaginable to the Boston fan. It was in this context that the Bruins arrived at the Boston Arena in the autumn of 1924.

It was the prospect of attracting the capacity crowds that supported Boston's local club and college teams that lured local businessman Charles F. Adams to invest in the first American NHL franchise. The Bruins were both an outgrowth of local tradition as well as a manifestation of the ambitions of the NHL. It was vital to the long-term growth of the sport and the league for it to sink solid roots in American soil. Boston was the perfect choice and has remained America's hockey hotbed for over a century.

The photographs in this, the first of a two-volume illustrated history, document both the success of Adams's investment as well as the achievements of the players that proudly wore the Bruins colors. These gentlemen comprised a portion of the most exclusive professional sporting club ever—namely, the old six-team, hundred-player National Hockey League. Their passion, commitment, and love of the game are evident on every page.

—Richard A. Johnson
September 2003

One

THE 1920s

THE BOSTON ARENA. For their first four seasons, the Bruins played their home games at the Boston Arena. The arena, built in 1910 within blocks of both the South End Grounds (Boston Braves) and Huntington Avenue Grounds (Red Sox), remains as one of the most historic sports venues in North America. Not only were the Bruins born here in 1924, but the Boston Celtics also played their first home game here in 1946. The arena, now known as Matthews Arena, also played host to the New England Whalers in 1973 and 1974 and is home to the Northeastern University Husky hockey and basketball teams. (Courtesy of Northeastern University Department of Athletics.)

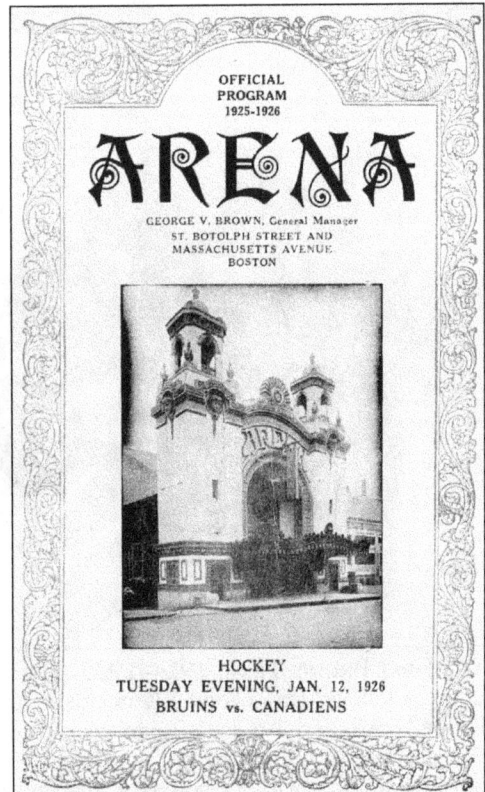

OFFICIAL
PROGRAM
1925-1926

ARENA

GEORGE V. BROWN, General Manager
ST. BOTOLPH STREET AND
MASSACHUSETTS AVENUE
BOSTON

HOCKEY
TUESDAY EVENING, JAN. 12, 1926
BRUINS vs. CANADIENS

CHARLES F. ADAMS. Charles F. Adams, a self-made grocery magnate and chairman of First National Stores, paid $15,000 to the NHL on November 1, 1924, for the rights to the first league franchise in the United States. One month to the day after paying the fee, his Bruins defeated the Montreal Maroons at the Boston Arena by a score of 2-1. (Collection of the Sports Museum, the Walter Brown Collection.)

THE FIRST BRUINS TEAM, 1924–1925. The members of the first Bruins team are, from left to right, as follows: (front row) Werner Schnarr, George Redding, Lloyd Cook, Carson Cooper, Bobby Rowe, and Art Ross (manager); (second row) Hec Fowler, Jimmy Herberts, Archie Skinner, Smokey Harris, Fern Headley, Herb Mitchell, and Tommy Murray (trainer). The team finished dead last with a record of 6 wins and 24 losses. (Collection of the Sports Museum.)

10

LIONEL HITCHMAN. Lionel Hitchman was a member of the original Bruins and arrived in Boston from the Ottawa Senators in a cash transaction. For 11 seasons, the defenseman, known to friends as "Fred," was often paired with Eddie Shore on defense and helped lead the Bruins to the 1929 Stanley Cup. The Bruins retired the No. 3 in his honor. (Collection of the Sports Museum.)

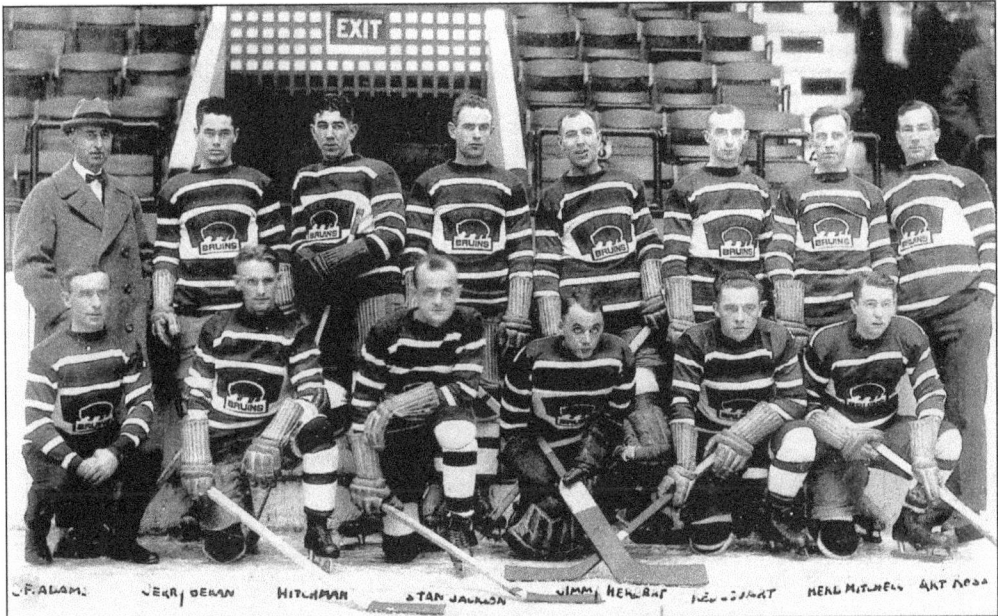

THE 1925–1926 BOSTON BRUINS. Seen here, from left to right, are the following: (front row) Thomas Murray, John Brackenbrough, Norm Shay, Charles Stewart, Carson Cooper, and George Redding; (back row) C.F. Adams (owner), George P. Geran, Lionel Hitchman, Stanley Jackson, Jimmy Herberts, William Stuart, Herb Mitchell, and Art Ross (manager). The Bruins fared better in their second season with a 17-15-4 record and a fourth-place finish. The team did not qualify for the Stanley Cup playoffs in the last season in which the playoffs were contested by both NHL and non-NHL teams.

ART ROSS. Art Ross was hockey's renaissance man. In his youth, Ross was considered one of the great all-around athletes in the province of Quebec as he excelled in hockey, lacrosse, baseball, soccer, and golf. As player-coach of the Montreal Wanderers, Ross designed the famed CH logo of the Montreal Canadiens. Bruins owner Charles F. Adams brought him to Boston in 1924 as both a partner and manager-coach of the fledgling Boston Bruins. He coached the team off and on into the 1940s and served as general manager until 1955. Among Ross's numerous contributions to hockey were the smooth-edged puck, the concave-shaped net, and the first metal hockey sticks. (Collection of the Sports Museum.)

SPRAGUE CLEGHORN, HAL WINKLER, AND LIONEL HITCHMAN, C. 1926. Burley enforcer Sprague Cleghorn bolstered a defense that featured goalie Hal Winkler (1.70 goals against average [GAA] in the 1926–1927 season) and fellow Hall of Famer Lionel Hitchman. Cleghorn served as Hitchman's defense partner until the arrival of Eddie Shore. Cleghorn, like Shore, was a tough customer whose temper cost him dearly in fines and suspensions. (Collection of the Sports Museum.)

12

THE 1926–1927 BOSTON BRUINS. From left to right are Hal Winkler, Sprague Cleghorn, Eddie Shore, Billy Coutu, Lionel Hitchman, Jim Herberts, Frank Frederickson, Percy Galbraith, Harry Oliver, Harry Meeking, and Bill "Red" Stuart. The 1926–1927 Bruins made it as far as the Stanley Cup finals, which they lost to the Ottawa Senators by two games to none with another two games that ended in ties. In the finals, Bruin defenseman Billy Coutu became the first NHL player to receive a lifetime suspension following his postgame assault on a referee. (Collection of the Sports Museum.)

AUBREY "DIT" CLAPPER. Dit Clapper arrived in Boston in 1927 as a high-scoring right winger and became the first NHL player to play 20 seasons (all with the Bruins), finishing his career as a defenseman in 1947. Not only was Clapper one of the biggest players of his era at six-feet-two-inches tall and 200 pounds, but he also commanded as much respect as his teammate Eddie Shore and was considered the heart and soul of the franchise. His No. 5 was retired by the team in his honor. (Collection of the Sports Museum.)

LIONEL HITCHMAN
Defense

HITCHMAN leaped into the world at Toronto, 25 years ago. At an early age he took to hockey with the Wychwood Club in Ontario. Hitchman has 10 years of hockey experience, having played with the Aura Lees, New Edinboro and Ottawa. He joined the Bruins two years ago and is one of the most versatile players in the league. Hitchman is a salesman in the off season, weighs 185 pounds and is known to the fans as "Hitch." He is No. 3.

CHARLES STEWART
Goal

CANADA made a great "save" when Dr. Charles Stewart entered the world at Carleton Place, Ontario, in 1895. Charlie has played hockey for 14 years. He has played with Kingston Collegiates, Frontenacs, Argonauts, Toronto Dentals, Aura Lees and Hamilton Tigers. This is Stewart's third year with the Bruins. "Doc" is one of the best goalies in hockey. He is a dentist and answers to "Doc." He is No. 11.

LIONEL HITCHMAN, CHARLES "DOC" STEWART, LELAND "HAGO" HARRINGTON, AND GORDON "DUKE" KEATS. These pages are from the Bruins 1926–1927 yearbook. (Collection of the Sports Museum, courtesy of the family of Herb Ralby.)

LELAND HARRINGTON
Wing

HAGO HARRINGTON is a native son, having been born in Melrose, Mass., in 1904. Harrington gained his first hockey experience as a member of the Melrose High School team, school champions. He then went with B. A. A. for two years and later was with Pere Marquette Club of Boston. This is Harrington's second season with the Bruins and his future is very promising. "Hago" conducts an ice business in the off season and weighs 158 pounds. He is No. 15.

GORDON KEATS
Center

DUKE KEATS was born in Montreal in 1897. He gained his first hockey experience ten years ago with the Cobalt Club and has since seen service with Toronto, and Edmonton. He is one of hockey's biggest men and is said to hold the puck longer than any man in the game. He was purchased this season by the Bruins from Edmonton. "Duke" is a fur buyer and weighs 195 pounds. He is No. 5.

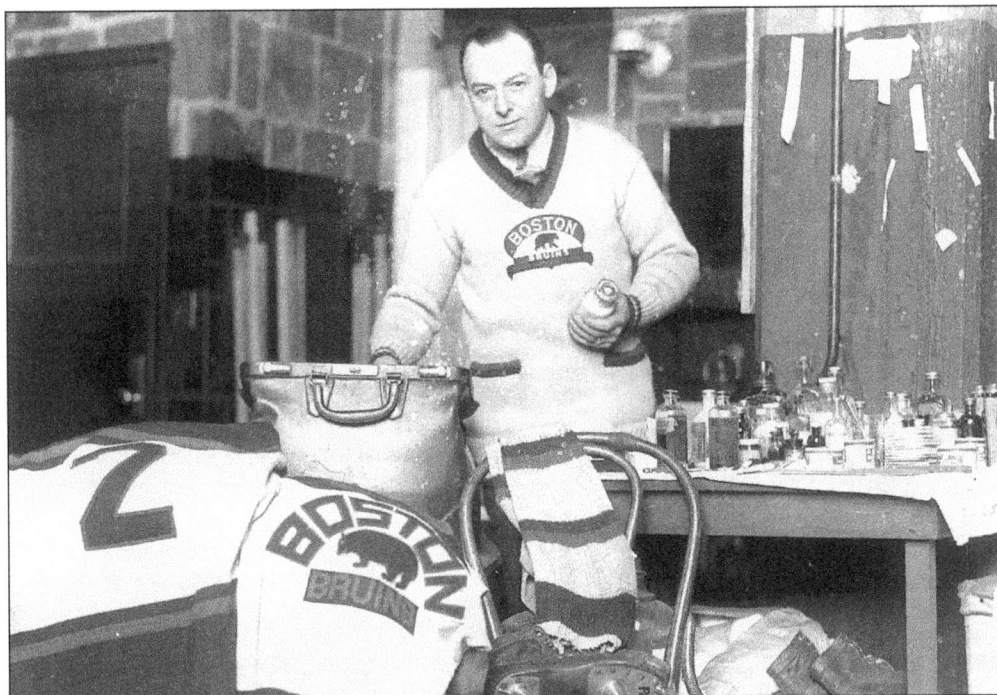

THE BRUINS TRAINER WIN GREEN. Win Green wore many hats as the trainer for the Bruins in the 1920s and 1930s. Not only did he tend to player injuries, but he also looked after the equipment and made sure that players' skates were sharpened as well. Typical of many trainers of his era, Green also served as the trainer for baseball's Boston Braves. (Collection of the Sports Museum.)

EDWARD SHORE
Defense

FORT QUEPPELL, Saskatchewan, claimed Shore as a native son in 1900. Shore's hockey experience has been in the West with the Manitoba Aggies, St. John's College, Indian Head Tigers, Melville Millionaires, Regina Capitals and Edmonton Eskimos. He is fast, rugged, and packs a great shot. His purchase by the Bruins was a ten-strike. Shore was called "The Galloping Cobweb" out West. He is an automobile salesman, weighs 185 pounds and likes to be called "Eddie." He is No. 2.

EDWARD SHORE. Another page from the Bruins 1926–1927 yearbook depicts Shore. (Collection of the Sports Museum, courtesy of the family of Herb Ralby.)

WILLIAM COUTU. Due to his brutal assault on a referee following a game against Ottawa in the 1927 Stanley Cup finals, Coutu was the first NHL player ever suspended for life. (Collection of the Sports Museum, courtesy of the family of Herb Ralby.)

WILLIAM COUTU
Defense

WILLIAM COUTU was born at North Bay, Ontario, in 1895. He has been playing professional hockey for nine years, having been with Soo St. Marie of Ontario, Hamilton, and *Les Canadiens. Coutu is a defense man par excellence and formerly teamed with "Peg" Cleghorn, Bruins captain when with the Canadiens. He was purchased this year by the Bruins from the Canadiens. Bill is a carpenter, weighs 190 pounds and pricks his ears to the name of "Beaver." He is No. 10.
*World's Champions

DIT CLAPPER, C. 1928. In 1928, coach Art Ross placed Clapper on a line with center Cooney Weiland and left wing Dutch Gainor, and the trio soon became known as the "Dynamite Line." The teammates took three of the top five team-scoring places and helped lead the Bruins to their first Stanley Cup in 1929. (Collection of the Sports Museum.)

PERCY "PERK" GALBRAITH.
World War I veteran Perk
Galbraith played left wing and
defense for the Bruins for eight
seasons, from 1926 to 1934. He
arrived from the Evelth-Hibbing
Rangers of the USA Hockey
Association and helped the
Bruins win their first Stanley
Cup in 1929. (Collection of the
Sports Museum.)

HARRY OLIVER. Hall of Famer Harry
Oliver led the Bruins in scoring
for three consecutive seasons, from
1926 through 1929. He remained
a consistent scorer for another five
seasons before being traded to the
New York Americans for cash on
November 2, 1934. (Collection of
the Sports Museum.)

POSITIVELY NO SMOKING DURING GAME

OFFICIAL
PROGRAM
1927-1928

ARENA

GEORGE V. BROWN
General Manager
ST. BOTOLPH ST.
AND
MASSACHUSETTS
AVENUE
BOSTON

BOSTON BRUINS
vs.
CANADIENS
TUESDAY
EVENING
DEC. 6, 1927
at 8.30 o'clock

A BOSTON ARENA PROGRAM. The Bruins called the Boston Arena home for four seasons before ticket demand and the overall growth of the NHL led the team to join with promoter Tex Rickard and sign on as the main tenant of the soon-to-be-constructed Boston Garden. (Courtesy of J. Harvey McKenney.)

THE DYNAMITE LINE: DIT CLAPPER, COONEY WEILAND, AND DUTCH GAINOR. The Dynamite Line experienced their greatest season in 1929–1930, when Weiland topped the league in scoring with 73 points and Clapper finished third with 61, a single point behind runner-up Frank Boucher of the Rangers. Weiland and Clapper led the league in goals scored with 43 and 41, respectively. Gainor was second in the league for assists with 31. (Courtesy of Mrs. Ralph Weiland.)

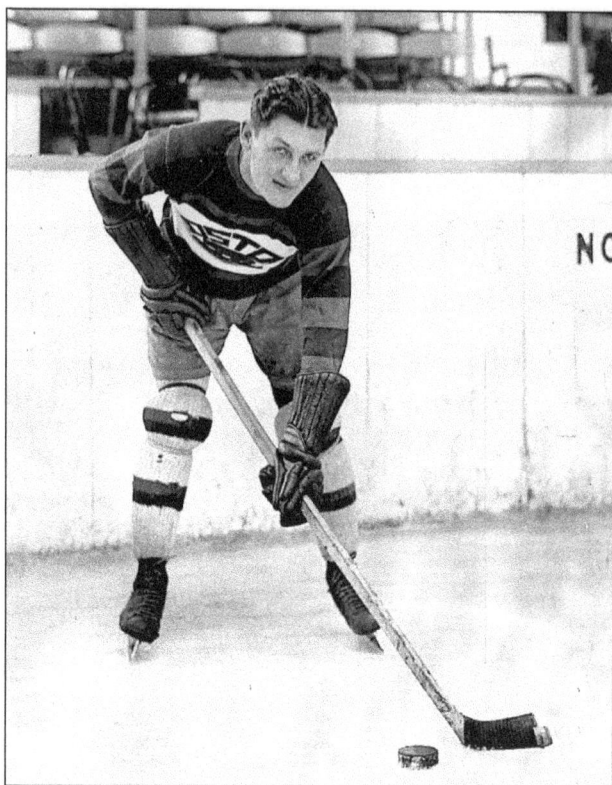

COONEY WEILAND. In the 1929–1930 season, the NHL made a significant rule change and allowed passing within the offensive zone. Forwards soon took advantage of the rule and virtually camped out in front of opposing nets awaiting passes. None took greater advantage than five-foot-seven-inch-tall, 150-pound center Cooney Weiland, who led the league in goals scored with 43 and overall points with 73. By December 21, the league modified the rule and created the modern offside rule that disallows offensive players to precede the puck over the blue line. (Collection of the Sports Museum.)

GEORGE OWEN. Former Harvard three-sport phenomenon George Owen signed with the Bruins for the highest bonus in NHL history to date in 1929 and played his first game with the team on January 8, 1929, in a 5-2 win over the Maple Leafs at the Boston Garden. The game was noteworthy in that Toronto owner Conn Smythe traveled with his team to Boston under the impression that the highly touted Owen would sign a contract with the Maple Leafs. Smythe was a good friend of Owen's father, who had designed a yacht for the Leafs' volatile owner. (Courtesy of George Owen.)

LIVELY LIVING LEGEND   By Vic Johnson

THIS CORNER WAS INTRIGUED BY THE NEWS STORY THAT A 70-YEAR-OLD FORMER BRUIN DEFENSE MAN PLAYED IN AN OLD-TIMERS GAME AT BRAINTREE, LAST FRIDAY NIGHT....

...BECAUSE WE REMEMBER HARVARD'S IMMORTAL **GEORGE OWEN** AS ONE OF THIS AREA'S MOST REMARKABLE ATHLETES

THE NEWTON NATIVE BURST UPON THE COLLEGIATE SCENE AS A TWO-WAY, 60-MINUTE, BACKFIELD ACE AT HARVARD IN 1920

OWEN CLIMAXED A BRILLIANT CAREER FOR THE CRIMSON WITH A TWO-OUT, 3 AND 2 COUNT, BASES-FULL, NINTH INNING HOME RUN TO BEAT YALE 8-7 IN 1923!

-HE HELPED OUR BRUINS WIN THEIR FIRST STANLEY CUP, IN 1929

GEORGE IS ONE OF ONLY FOUR MEN EVER TO WIN NINE HARVARD VARSITY LETTERS

20

EDDIE SHORE, GEORGE OWEN, AND LIONEL HITCHMAN. George Owen proved to be the final component of the Bruins Stanley Cup master plan in 1929. Owen, a local hero and graduate of both Newton High and Harvard, joined the Bruins as a 27-year-old rookie and helped lead them to their first Stanley Cup victory over the Montreal Canadiens. Owen later succeeded Hitchman as the Bruins second-ever captain in 1931. (Collection of the Sports Museum.)

BOSTON BRUINS
WORLD CHAMPIONS
Stanley Cup Winners
AMERICAN DIVISION CHAMPIONS · PRINCE OF WALES TROPHY WINNERS
SEASON 1928-29

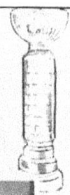

'DUTCH'KLEIN 'BILL CARSON GEO. OWEN HARRY OLIVER WIN GREEN.forward MYLES LANE NORMAN 'DUTCH' GAINOR AUBREY DIT CLAPPER
PERCY GALBRAITH EDDIE SHORE 'MICKEY' McKAY ART ROSS, mgr FRED HITCHMAN CY DENNENY RALPH 'COONEY' WEILAND
'TINY' THOMPSON

Charles F. Adams, PRESIDENT
Arthur H. Ross, VICE PRES & GEN. MGR.

Ralph F. Burkard, TREASURER
Frank Ryan, PUBLICITY DIRECTOR

THE BOSTON BRUINS 1928–1929 STANLEY CUP CHAMPIONS. The 1928–1929 Stanley Cup champions defeated the Montreal Canadiens and the New York Rangers in a five-game undefeated sweep of the playoffs. (Collection of the Sports Museum.)

BOSTON GARDEN NEWS
Season of 1932-1933
Editors — FRED HOEY — "LES" STOUT

BOSTON GARDEN OFFICERS

JOSEPH T. GILMAN, President, Boston
WILLIAM F. CAREY, Treasurer, New York
LIEUT.-GEN. EDWARD L. LOGAN, Secretary, Boston

DIRECTORS
JOHN R. MACOMBER, Chairman

WILLIAM J. BINGHAM
MATHEW C. BRUSH
WILLIAM F. CAREY
EDWARD S. FRENCH

GEORGE V. FUNK
JOSEPH T. GILMAN
HUNTINGTON R. HARDWICK
RICHARD F. HOYT

JOHN S. LAWRENCE
LOUIS K. LIGGETT
LT.-GEN. EDWARD L. LOGAN
HOMER LORING

MAJOR P. F. O'KEEFE
THOMAS NELSON PERKINS
LESTER WATSON
ROBERT S. WEEKS

WILLIAM J. BINGHAM
HUNTINGTON R. HARDWICK

EXECUTIVE COMMITTEE
MAJOR P. F. O'KEEFE, Chairman
WILLIAM F. CAREY
HOMER LORING

GEORGE C. FUNK
LESTER WATSON

THE BOSTON GARDEN. The Boston Garden served as home to the Bruins from 1928 to 1995. For most of their games, the figure 13,909, the capacity for a hockey sellout, accompanied game scorecards. (Collection of the Sports Museum.)

Two

THE 1930s

EDDIE SHORE AND FANS, 1934. He may have been hated and feared by opponents, but the fans in Boston loved Eddie Shore. Here, he takes time to sign some autographs along the boards. (Collection of the Sports Museum, photograph by Leslie Jones.)

ART ROSS AND SONS, 1930. Hockey appears to run in the family as Art Ross poses with his sons John, 11, and Art Jr., 13. (Collection of the Sports Museum, photograph by Leslie Jones.)

EDDIE SHORE AND CHARLES F. ADAMS, 1934. Charles F. Adams purchased an entire league to obtain the services of Eddie Shore in 1926. Unlike many players of the era, Shore had the clout to hold out for more money when it came time to ink a new deal, and he frequently did. He was too valuable to sit on the sidelines, so he usually got what he wanted. (Collection of the Sports Museum.)

COONEY WEILAND SPINS SOME
PLATTERS AT THE GARDEN, 1931.
Ralph "Cooney" Weiland played
on two Stanley Cup teams (1929
and 1939) and coached one (1941).
Note the position of the elbow
pads. It was not until the 1940s that
they were worn under the jersey.
(Collection of the Sports Museum,
photograph by Leslie Jones.)

THE 1930–1931 BRUINS. Still clad in brown and gold, this team featured many players from the
1929 Stanley Cup championship team as well as many who would play on the 1939 Stanley Cup
team. From left to right are the following: (front row) Harry Oliver, Dit Clapper, Jack Pratt, Eddie
Shore, Tiny Thompson, Lionel Hitchman, George Owen, Marty Barry, and Perk Galbraith; (back
row) Hal Darragh, Art Chapman, Red Beattie, Art Ross, Cooney Weiland, Smokey Harris, and
Dutch Gainor. (Collection of the Sports Museum, photograph by Leslie Jones.)

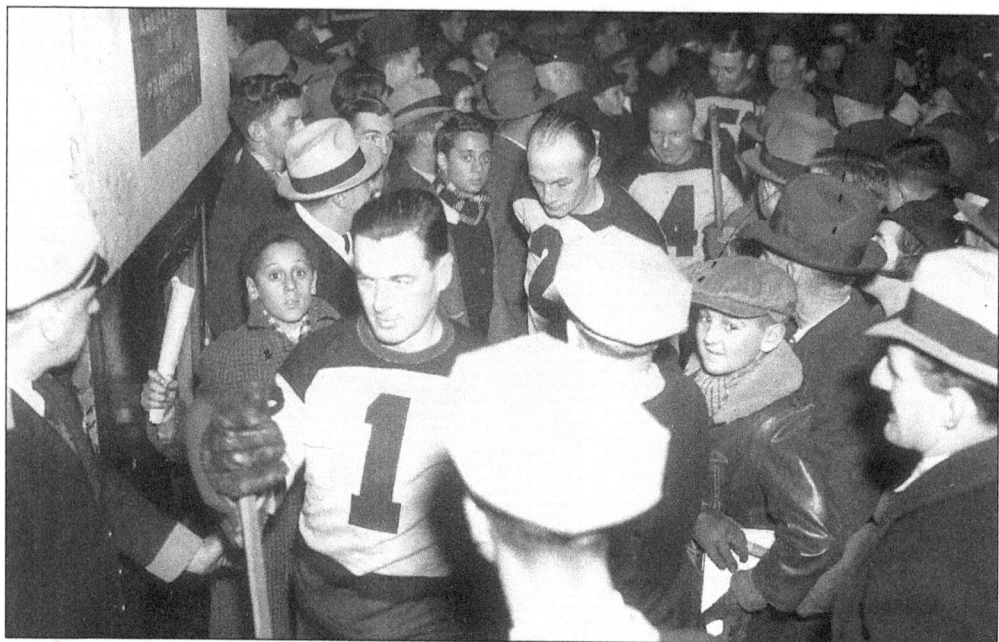

THE BRUINS TAKE THE ICE. It was a Bruin tradition in the 1930s to take the ice in numerical order. The position of the locker room was such that the players passed through the crowd of adoring fans, giving the Garden crowd an up-close and personal look at their heroes. Tiny Thompson (1) is followed by Eddie Shore (2), Red Beattie (4), and Dit Clapper (5). (Photograph by Leslie Jones, collection of the Sports Museum.)

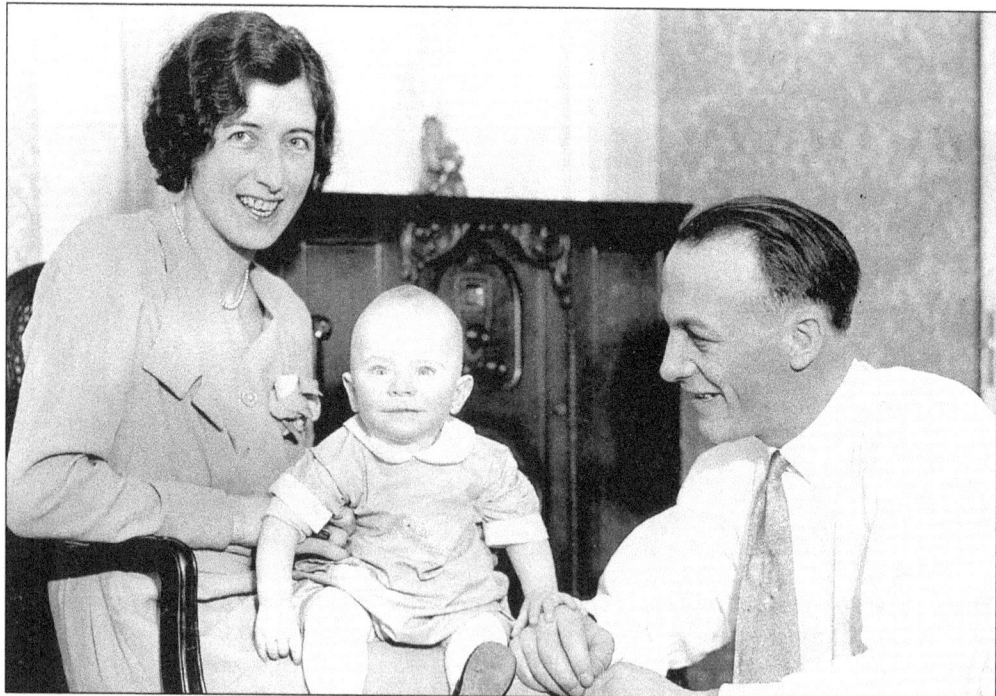

THE SHORES. Catherine, Teddy, and Eddie Shore pose for photographers in their Brookline apartment. (Collection of the Sports Museum.)

26

A U.S. Navy Airship Passes over Boston Garden. Tucked in between the Hotel Manger, the office building at 150 Causeway Street, and the elevated railway (later the MBTA), the Boston Garden nonetheless stood out with its tall spires and illuminated "Boston Garden North Station" sign. The Garden was home to the Bruins for 67 seasons, from 1928 until the end of the 1994–1995 season. These years included five Stanley Cups, countless playoff games, and hundreds of players. The Garden was cozy, as its ice surface was 15 feet shorter than regulation length. It also was built above a train station, and players claimed to have felt the ice vibrate with the movement of outbound and inbound trains while standing at attention for the national anthem. A symbol of 1930s technical progress, a U.S. Navy dirigible drifts overhead in this image. (Courtesy of the New Boston Garden Corporation.)

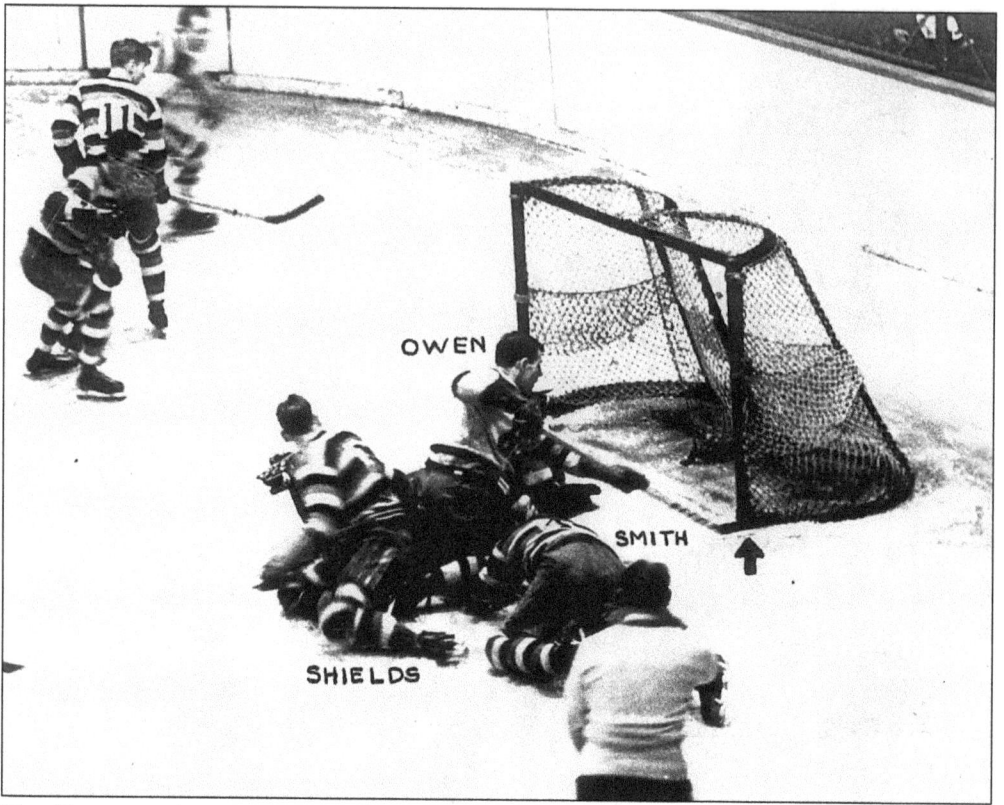

THE BRUINS IN ACTION AGAINST OTTAWA, 1933. In this rare action shot, the Bruins' George Owen crashes the Ottawa net to score. (Collection of the Boston Public Library.)

TINY THOMPSON BY BOB COYNE, 1938. Sports cartoonists of the era told a whole story in a single drawing. The small insets were a trademark of such artists as Bob Coyne and Gene Mack. (Collection of the Sports Museum, Milt Schmidt Archive.)

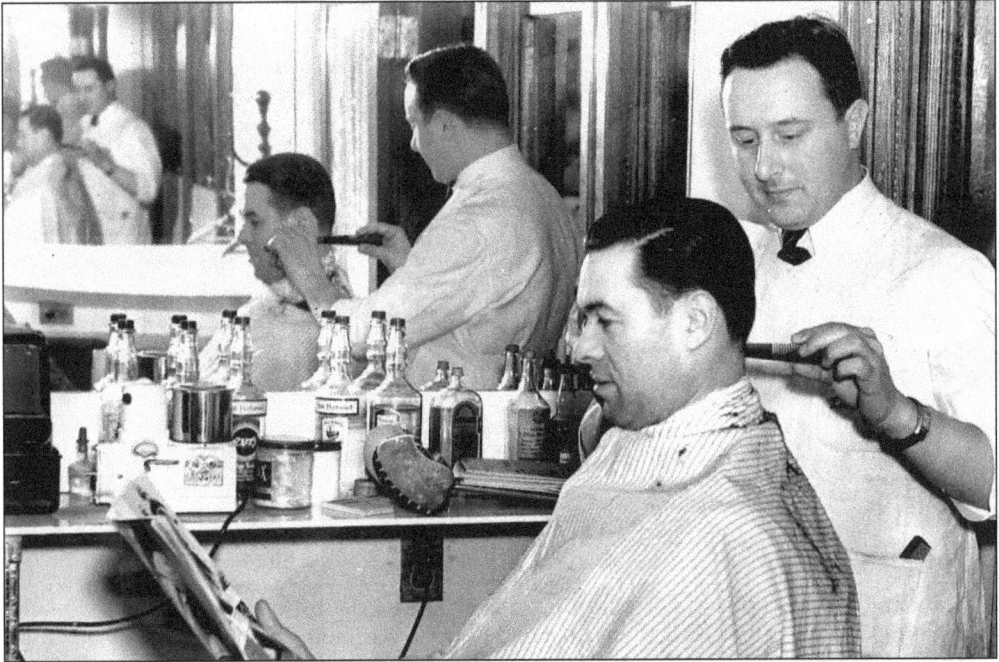

TINY THOMPSON, 1938. The leading goalie in the league takes time out for a haircut from barber Joe Drago. Fancy hotels of the era always had a barbershop, shoeshine stand, and laundry service to keep their patrons looking their best. (Photograph by Leslie Jones, Milt Schmidt Archive.)

TINY THOMPSON AND EDDIE SHORE. Stars Tiny Thompson and Eddie Shore model their dapper street clothes in the Bruins locker room. Both Bruin veterans by the 1930s, they were a major reason the Bruins won the Stanley Cup in 1929. Shore was still there to win again in 1939, but Thompson was traded to Detroit early in the 1938–1939 season. (Collection of the Sports Museum, photograph by Leslie Jones.)

THE SHORE-BAILEY INCIDENT, DECEMBER 12, 1933. The battles between the Bruins and Maple Leafs during the Great Depression were fierce, but none was more competitive or bloody than that played on December 12, 1933, at Boston Garden. While leading a rush toward the Toronto goal, Bruin defenseman Eddie Shore was tripped by Leaf defenseman King Clancy. When Shore saw that no penalty was called, he sped toward the first Toronto player he spied—Ace Bailey. Shore launched a devastating hit on Bailey, knocking the Leaf forward onto the ice. Bailey lay motionless as Shore was accosted first by Toronto captain and enforcer Red Horner and later by other Leaf players. Shore, not recognizing the damage he had done to Bailey, grinned back at Horner, prompting the defenseman to level him with one punch that sent the Bruin to the ice unconscious. For days, Bailey hovered near death and was operated on twice to relieve pressure in his skull. He eventually recovered but never played hockey again. Shore received a 16-game suspension and the lasting enmity of fans across North America. (Collection of the Sports Museum.)

PUBLIC ENEMY NUMBER ONE. They did not come any tougher than Eddie Shore. Among the numerous stories of Shore's ability to absorb suffering as well as dole it out is the time his ear was nearly severed in a collision at a Bruins practice. In the beginning of the 1926–1927 season, another notoriously rough player, Billy Coutu, hit Shore hard, smashing his own forehead against the side of Shore's skull. The collision nearly sheared off Shore's ear, which dangled by a bit of flesh. Told by the team doctor that the ear would be lost, Shore held it against his head and went looking for a second opinion. He visited several doctors near the Garden who all wanted to amputate the ear. Finally, Shore found a doctor who agreed to try to save it. Upon being offered an anesthetic, Shore refused, saying, "Just give me a mirror, I want to make sure you sew it on straight." The doctor was able to save the ear, adding to the legend as well as to the over 900 stitches that Shore's body took during his career. (Collection of the Sports Museum.)

ACE BAILEY AND EDDIE SHORE AT THE ACE BAILEY BENEFIT GAME. On February 14, 1934, the Maple Leafs played a team of NHL All-Stars (including Eddie Shore) as a benefit for the stricken Ace Bailey. Here, Bailey (in street clothes) greets Shore prior to the game. In future years, Bailey worked as an official at Maple Leaf Gardens. Both men are enshrined at the Hockey Hall of Fame. (Collection of the Sports Museum.)

THE BRUINS LOCKER ROOM, 1934. Trainer Win Green and an unidentified assistant distribute refreshments to Bruins players between periods. It was a time before Gatorade or energy drinks, when refreshment meant water, fruit, or ice. Red Beattie, behind Dit Clapper, munches an orange. (Photograph by Leslie Jones.)

ART ROSS AND EDDIE SHORE. Eddie Shore was the kind of hockey player Art Ross had in mind for the Bruins: tough, hard hitting, and fearless. One time, Shore missed the team train to Montreal. Rather than miss the game, he borrowed a limousine and chauffeur from a friend and headed north. Driving through the night over winding country roads, the snowfall worsened into a blizzard and the terrified driver refused to go on, so Shore took the wheel. When the windshield wipers failed, Shore drove with the window open, brushing the snow away with his left hand while steering with his right. Four times the car skidded off the road and Shore and the driver got it out. The fifth time, they ended up in a ditch. Shore had to hike to a nearby farm and borrow a team of horses to get it out. They finally arrived in Montreal at 5:30 p.m., giving Shore just enough time for dinner and a nap before the game. The exhausted, frostbitten defenseman played the entire game and scored the game-winning goal. Despite Shore's extraordinary effort, Art Ross fined him for missing the train. (Photograph by Leslie Jones.)

OFF DUTY, 1935. Dit Clapper, Marty Barry, Tiny Thompson, and Max Kaminsky admire a decoy, perhaps thinking of off-season hunting trips to come. (Photograph by Leslie Jones.)

THE 1934–1935 BRUINS. This unusual shot shows the 1934–1935 Bruins lining up for their official team picture. From left to right are the following: (front row) Tiny Thompson, Eddie Shore, Art Ross, Weston Adams, Frank Patrick, Nels Stewart, and Dit Clapper; (second row) Bert McInenly, Red Beattie, Jerry Shannon, Win Green, Peggy O'Neil, Max Kaminsky, and Marty Barry; (third row) Jack Shill, Pinky Davie, Alex Motter, Jack Portland, Babe Siebert, Charlie Sands, and Paul Haynes. (Collection of the Boston Public Library.)

BILL COWLEY, 1938. Bill Cowley began his professional career with the St. Louis Eagles (1934–1935) but was claimed by the Bruins in a dispersal draft when the Eagles folded after only one season. Although the Bruins had the sixth pick, the underrated rookie turned out to be a wise choice. A two-time Hart Trophy winner (1941 and 1943), Cowley won the Art Ross Trophy in 1941 and the Dufresne Trophy in 1944. He played on two Stanley Cup teams (1939 and 1941) and was elected to the Hockey Hall of Fame in 1968. (Photograph by Leslie Jones.)

34

ART ROSS AND BILL STEWART, 1938. After the last game of the 1937–1938 season, Art Ross points toward Toronto, where the Bruins were heading, while Bill Stewart of Chicago hitches a thumb toward Montreal, where his team would play. Stewart's Blackhawks went on to win the Stanley Cup, making him the first American coach to achieve that feat. (Collection of the Sports Museum.)

EDDIE SHORE, 1936. Dressed in street clothes, Eddie Shore chats with Bruin players Flash Hollett, Sylvio Mantha, Allan Shields, and Jack Portland. (Photograph by Leslie Jones.)

TAKING A BREAK ALONG THE BOARDS, 1937. Roy Goldsworthy, Cooney Weiland, and Red Beattie take a break to discuss game strategy. Goldsworthy and Beattie were gone from the club before they won the Stanley Cup in 1939. (Photograph by Leslie Jones.)

ART ROSS AND COONEY WEILAND, 1938. Manager Art Ross congratulates his new assistant manger. Weiland played on the 1929 and 1938 Stanley Cup teams and eventually coached another one in 1941. Weiland later was named hockey coach at Harvard, where he coached such players as Bobby Bauer Jr. and the Cleary brothers. (Photograph by Leslie Jones.)

THE BRUINS PRACTICE, 1938. Bill Cowley and Roy Conacher take a break from practice to talk to coach Art Ross. (Photograph by Leslie Jones.)

JEAN PUSIE, 1935. One of the most colorful players in team history, defenseman Jean Pusie wrestled bears in carnivals in his home province of Quebec as his off-season job. He played one season in Boston, 1934–1935. (Photograph by Leslie Jones.)

THE 1937–1938 BRUINS. The 1937–1938 Bruins were a year away from their first Stanley Cup since 1929. From left to right are Jack Portland, Gord Pettinger, Dit Clapper, Flash Hollett, Woody Dumart, Roy Goldsworthy, Milt Schmidt, Ray Getliffe, Charlie Sands, Eddie Shore, Bill

Cowley, Tiny Thompson, Art Jackson, Cooney Weiland, and Bobby Bauer. All but Thompson, Jackson, and Goldsworthy would play on the 1939 championship team. (Collection of the Sports Museum.)

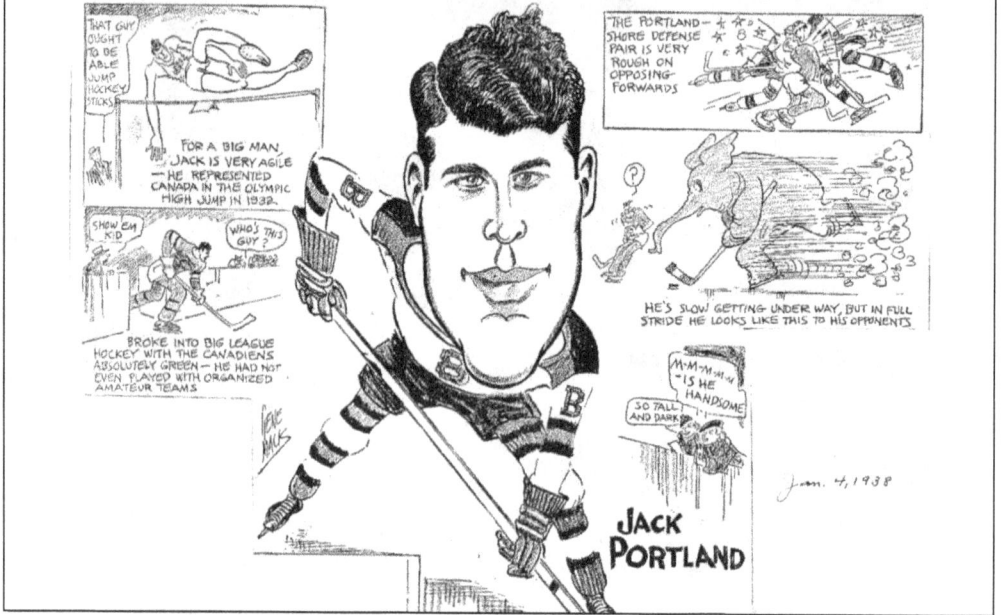

Eddie Shore's Defense Partner . . . . By Gene Mack

JACK PORTLAND

JACK PORTLAND BY GENE MACK, 1938. Affable and smiling off the ice, the six-foot-two-inch Portland was teamed up with Eddie Shore to make sure no one got near Tiny Thompson's goal. Gene Mack, born Eugene McGillicuddy in North Cambridge, Massachusetts, was a distant relative of baseball's Connie Mack. More than any other cartoonist of the day, Gene Mack used small sketches around the main picture to tell the story of a player's life or of the previous night's game. Mack was a master of making even the tiniest simple sketch recognizable as a player, coach, or public figure. (Collection of the Sports Museum, Milt Schmidt Archive.)

Shifting Sands! -:- -:- *By Bob Coyne*

CHARLIE SANDS

CHARLIE SANDS BY BOB COYNE, 1938. The usually astute Conn Smythe let a big one get away when he traded Charlie Sands to Boston for cash in 1934. The hard-hitting forward played on the 1939 Stanley Cup team before he was traded to Montreal for Herb Cain. (Collection of the Sports Museum, Milt Schmidt Archive.)

THOMPSON TRADED! On November 16, 1938, Boston fans were stunned to discover that veteran goalie Cecil "Tiny" Thompson had been traded to Detroit. Thompson had backstopped the Bruins to a Stanley Cup in 1929, his first season with the club. A multiple all-star and winner of the Vezina Trophy in 1930, 1933, 1936, and 1938, Thompson was immensely popular with the fans. He was replaced in net by a young Minnesotan named Frank Brimsek, who would himself lead the Bruins to the Stanley Cup in his first season. (Collection of the Sports Museum, Milt Schmidt Archive.)

'TINY' THOMPSON SOLD BY BRUINS

STORY ON PAGE 3

Tiny Goes West—Sold to Detroit's Red Wings for the tidy sum of $15,000 is Bruin Goalie Tiny Thompson, shown with

THE BRUINS SKATE OUT FOR WARM UPS, 1939. Frank Brimsek steps out on the ice, followed by Eddie Shore. Although Tiny Thompson had been one of the premier goaltenders of the 1930s, the decision to go with Brimsek in 1938 proved to be a good one. Thompson finished his career with the Red Wings two years later. Brimsek played for the Bruins until 1949, backstopping the team to Stanley Cups in 1939 and 1941. (Photograph by Leslie Jones.)

41

A Mighty Handy Guy! -:- By Bob Coyne

RAY GETLIFFE

RAY GETLIFFE BY BOB COYNE, 1938. Getliffe came to the Bruins on December 31, 1935. He became a regular in the 1936–1937 season, playing on the 1939 Stanley Cup team. Traded to Montreal, he played for Les Habitants through the war years, picking up another Stanley Cup in 1944. (Collection of the Sports Museum, Milt Schmidt Archive.)

RELAXING IN THE DINING CAR, 1938. In the days of train travel, passengers took time to relax in the dining car. Here, Woody Dumart and Flash Hollett eat while Bill Cowley and Dit Clapper chat in the background. (Collection of the Sports Museum.)

42

ART ROSS BY BOB COYNE, 1938. According to this cartoon, Art Ross was the sparkplug that ignited the Bruins. After coming to the Bruins in 1924, Ross began to build a competitive team in his own image. He was inducted into the Hockey Hall of Fame in 1945. (Collection of the Sports Museum, Milt Schmidt Archive.)

ACTION AT THE GARDEN, 1938–1939. Brimsek smothers the puck as Bruin and Maple Leaf players look on. Note that two Bruins, including Eddie Shore (2), are wearing helmets. Goalie masks, however, were just a distant dream. (Photograph by Leslie Jones.)

"They Shall Not Pass!" -:- By Bob Coyne

FRANK BRIMSEK BY BOB COYNE, 1938. The new Bruin goaltender had a lot to prove when he came to Boston in 1938. Happy in Providence, Brimsek was reluctant to come to the big club but soon proved that he was more than up to the task. He won the Calder Trophy as rookie of the year and backstopped the Bruins to the Stanley Cup. (Collection of the Sports Museum, Milt Schmidt Archive.)

"MR. ZERO." Frank Brimsek had big skates to fill when he came to Boston to replace the immensely popular Tiny Thompson. He more than exceeded fan expectations, posting six shutouts in his first eight games and breaking the record for consecutive scoreless minutes with 321 minutes and 54 seconds. This remarkable feat earned him the nickname Mr. Zero. (Photograph by Leslie Jones.)

44

BANANAS SCORE HIGH WITH BOSTON BRUINS

Athletes here eat popular fruit for quick food energy

IT'S A TOP SCORE FRUIT, agree these three famous Bruins, Bill Cowley, sensational new center, Cecil "Tiny" Thompson, all-star goalie, and Ralph "Cooney" Weiland, veteran Bruins defense man and winner of the Hart trophy, munches a banana while he looks on from the sideline. Bananas are recommended for training table diets because they easily digested sugars are a source of food energy.

THE BRUINS GO BANANAS. "Bananas score high with Boston Bruins" shouts this headline, as though announcing V-J Day. Bananas were just coming into their own in the American diet and were touted as "quick energy food." Bill Cowley, Tiny Thompson, and Cooney Weiland chow down on the wonder fruit while Eddie Shore, shown in the inset, has clearly been retouched to express his banana-eating pleasure. (Collection of the Sports Museum, Milt Schmidt Archive.)

It Costs $135.75 to Equip a Goali

SUSPENDERS $1.25

SHOULDER PADS $11

BODY PAD $8.50

SWEATER $6

ELBOW $6.50

GLOVES $10.75

PANTS $5.50

SHIN PADS $45

STICK $3.75

SOCKS $2.50

SKATES $35

...k Brimsek of Boston Bruins shows what well-dressed h...
goalie is wearing . . . . and what it cost...

EQUIPPING A GOALIE, 1939. The goaltender is the most expensive player on the ice to dress. In 1939, it cost a whopping $135.75 to equip a goalie, from his $6.00 jersey to his $35.00 skates. Pads for NHL goaltenders at the time were custom made and were often worn for an entire career. (Collection of the Sports Museum, Milt Schmidt Archive.)

RAY GETLIFFE. Center and left wing Ray Getliffe played for the Bruins from 1935 through the Stanley Cup season of 1938–1939. Getliffe scored 37 goals for Boston before being traded to the Montreal Canadiens along with forward Charlie Sands for center Herb Cain. (Collection of the Sports Museum.)

THE SHORES AT HOME. Eddie Shore did have a domestic side. Here, he poses with his wife, Catherine, and son, Teddy, in their Brookline apartment. Catherine, a world-class basketball player in her own right, attended every home game and often tended Shore's wounds. (Photograph by Leslie Jones.)

46

A One-Man Hockey Team! Bob Coyne's 1938 cartoon hails high-scoring center Bill Cowley as a one-man team. A deft playmaker and prolific scorer, Cowley played on two Stanley Cup teams in his career in Boston. (Collection of the Sports Museum, Milt Schmidt Archive.)

A One-Man Hockey Team! -:- By Bob Coyne

Flash Hollett. William "Flash" Hollett came to the Bruins by way of the Toronto Maple Leafs in 1936. The big defenseman was good with his stick, both with the puck and against opposing players. He played on the Stanley Cup teams of 1939 and 1941 before being traded to Detroit for Pat Egan in 1944. (Photograph by Leslie Jones.)

47

THE KRAUT LINE IN ACTION, 1939. The Bruins take on Toronto as the puck gets away from Milt Schmidt (15) and two unidentified Leafs. Woody Dumart (14) and Bobby Bauer (17) of

the Kraut Line are joined by Flash Hollett (12). (Photograph by Leslie Jones.)

ART FOR ART ROSS'S SAKE BY GENE MACK, 1938. A thinking man's hockey player, Bobby Bauer always seemed to be in the right place at the right time. He was, in the eyes of Gene Mack and Boston fans, a classic in every way. (Collection of the Sports Museum, Milt Schmidt Archive.)

ART ROSS BY GENE MACK, 1938. Bruins mastermind Art Ross bangs the boards to signal his players in this 1939 cartoon. Not only a keen judge of talent, Ross was also a master of strategy and line changing. (Collection of the Sports Museum, Milt Schmidt Archive.)

ACTION AT THE GARDEN. Milt Schmidt (15) and Bobby Bauer (17) press the attack against Maple Leaf goalie Turk Broda. (Photograph by Leslie Jones.)

EDDIE SHORE IN THE LOCKER ROOM. Described as cold, aloof, and a loner off the ice, Eddie Shore was something of an enigma to his teammates. On the ice, however, he played with a passion that was unmatched in the sport. (Photograph by Leslie Jones.)

THE SUDDEN DEATH KID! "Sudden Death" Mel Hill performed the amazing feat of scoring three overtime goals in the 1939 playoff series with the New York Rangers. (Collection of the Sports Museum, Milt Schmidt Archive.)

FRANK CALDER PRESENTS A 1939 STANLEY CUP MEDALLION. Eddie Shore receives his 1939 Stanley Cup medallion from league president Frank Calder at the Boston Garden. (Collection of the Sports Museum.)

BRUINS PLAYERS ON THE STAIRS IN THE GARDEN. Sporting a variety of team jackets, the Bruins pose for photographer Leslie Jones in one of the Boston Garden stairwells. These jackets, available to the players in a choice of leather or cloth, commemorate the 1938–1939 and the 1939–1940 seasons. Note the rodeo pictures on the wall to the left. From left to right are the

following: (front row) Johnny Crawford (standing), Milt Schmidt (seated), Bobby Bauer, and Woody Dumart; (back row) Flash Hollett, Eddie Wiseman, Frank Brimsek, Roy Conacher, Jack Shewchuk, and Dit Clapper. (Photograph by Leslie Jones.)

BRINGING BACK THE CUP, 1941. Johnny Crawford and captain Dit Clapper show Bill Cowley the Stanley Cup as they arrive at the Huntington Avenue station (the injured Cowley did not make the trip). About 300 fans were on hand to greet the boys as they returned from Detroit after sweeping the Red Wings in the finals. Note that the cup is missing its base. The Stanley Cup is actually just the bowl; the trophy we know today is the newest in a series in which bases are added to accommodate the names and rosters of the winning teams. The cup itself predates the NHL. It was donated by Lord Stanley of Preston as a challenge cup in 1893. Ironically, Lord Stanley never saw a contest for the trophy that bears his name. (Collection of the Sports Museum.)

WESTON ADAMS AND EDDIE SHORE, 1938. President Weston Adams welcomes Eddie Shore back into the fold after a contract holdout. Fittingly, the photograph opportunity took place in Trophy Corner in the Bruins offices. (Collection of the Sports Museum.)

Three

THE 1940S

MILT SCHMIDT AND TEEDER KENNEDY. On the ice it was all business, but on the boards, captains Milt Schmidt and Ted "Teeder" Kennedy could enjoy a laugh. (Collection of the Sports Museum.)

FAREWELL TO THE KRAUTS, 1942. As World War II escalated in Europe, the Kraut Line joined the Royal Canadian Air Force. In their last game before going off to war, Bobby Bauer, Milt Schmidt, and Woody Dumart, pictured from left to right, collected three goals and eight assists.

After a presentation, both the Garden faithful and players from the Bruins and Canadiens carried the boys off the ice on their shoulders. (Collection of the Sports Museum.)

FRANK CALDER AND DIT CLAPPER, 1940. NHL president Frank Calder presents Bruins captain Dit Clapper with a medal emblematic of the league championship before the season opener. The Bruins won the Stanley Cup the previous spring. (Collection of the Sports Museum.)

BILL COWLEY, 1941. Bill Cowley held the highest points per game total for one season with 1.97 in 1943–1944, until Wayne Gretzky topped it in the 1980–1981 season. During that season, Cowley scored an amazing 71 points in just 36 games. (Collection of the Sports Museum.)

DR. MARTIN CROTTY AND BILL COWLEY, 1941. Team doctor Martin Crotty greets frequent patient Bill Cowley. A great playmaker, it was said that Cowley "made more wings than Boeing." A two-time Hart Trophy winner (1941 and 1943), he won the Art Ross Trophy in 1941 and the Dufresne Trophy in 1944. Cowley played on two Stanley Cup teams (1939 and 1941) and was elected to the Hockey Hall of Fame in 1968. (Collection of the Sports Museum.)

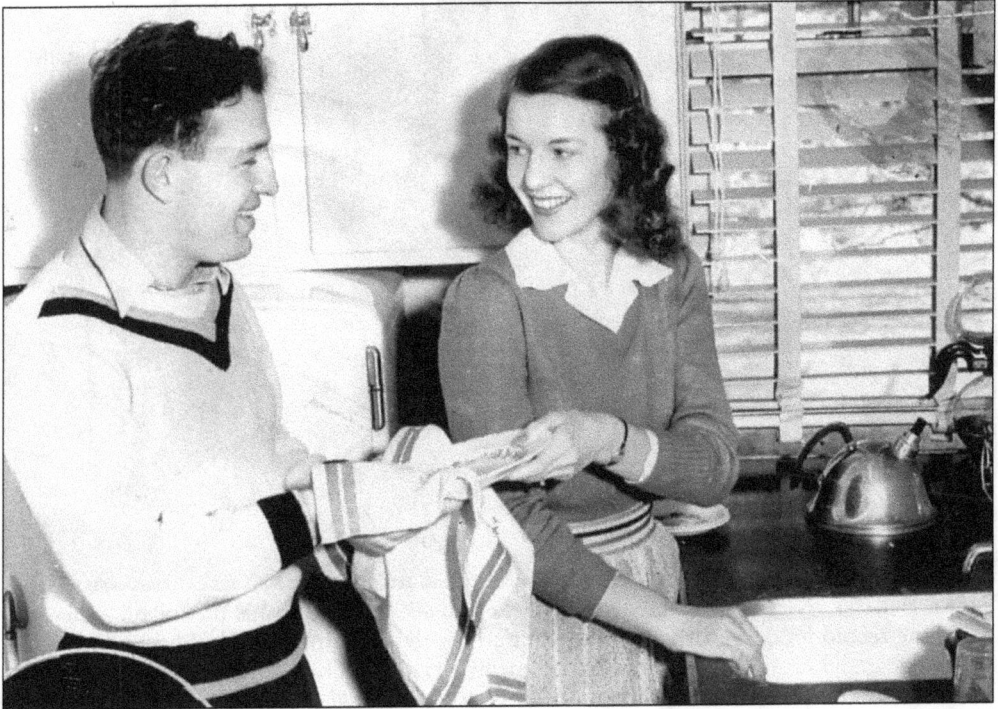

AT HOME WITH THE BAUERS, 1942. Bobby Bauer helps with the dishes. Bauer's beautiful bride was a member of the Bauer sporting goods company (no relation to Bobby). When Bauer retired from hockey in 1947, he moved to Toronto and went to work for the company. (Collection of the Sports Museum.)

FRANK BRIMSEK. Nicknamed Mr. Zero, Brimsek had six shutouts in his first eight games and broke the record for consecutive scoreless minutes with 321 minutes and 54 seconds. He was an American, hailing from Eveleth, Minnesota, an NHL rarity in those days. In his first season, he led the Bruins to the Stanley Cup, won the Vezina and Calder Trophies, and was named to the NHL All-Star team. He won the Dufresne Trophy in 1943 and 1948. He also played on the 1941 Stanley Cup team. Brimsek played his final season with Chicago (1949–1950) and was elected to the Hockey Hall of Fame in 1966. (Collection of the Sports Museum.)

ART ROSS SR. AND JR., 1940. Art Ross and son Art Jr. take a breather during a golf game. During World War II, Art Jr. joined the Royal Canadian Air Force and saw combat action in Europe. He was captured and escaped twice from German POW camps. (Collection of the Sports Museum.)

ART ROSS AND SONS, 1942. Art Ross poses proudly with his two sons. At the time this picture was taken, Art Jr. (in uniform) served as a pilot officer in the Royal Canadian Air Force and John was training to be a pilot. (Collection of the Sports Museum.)

DIT CLAPPER. As the top policeman in the NHL, Clapper gave the needed protection and guidance to his younger teammates. Generations of Bruins benefited from his experience, enthusiasm, and friendship. (Collection of the Sports Museum.)

MILT SCHMIDT, COONEY WEILAND, AND BILL COWLEY, 1941. Coach Ralph "Cooney" Weiland confers with lamplighters Milt Schmidt and Bill Cowley. The Bruins would win the Stanley Cup that spring. The Bruins occasionally wore these unusual gold sweaters with a script logo in the early 1940s. (Photograph by Leslie Jones.)

THE **1941 STANLEY CUP TEAM.** From left to right are the following: (front row) Frank Brimsek, Bill Cowley, John Crawford, Cooney Weiland (coach), Art Ross (manager), Dit Clapper, Milt Schmidt, Woody Dumart, and Bobby Bauer; (back row) Art Jackson, Mel Hill, Des Smith, Roy

Conacher, Win Green (trainer), Flash Hollett, Jack Shewchuk, Red Hamill, Herb Cain, and Eddie Wiseman. Many of the players on this club were also on the 1939 Stanley Cup team. (Collection of the Sports Museum.)

THE KRAUT LINE, 1941. In 1936, rookie Milt Schmidt (center) joined his boyhood friend Woody Dumart (right) in Boston. A year later, Schmidt and Dumart were joined by another Kitchener native, Bobby Bauer (left), and together they formed the Kraut Line. They played together, lived together, received the same salary to the penny, and even went to war together until Bauer's retirement in 1947. (Collection of the Sports Museum.)

THE KRAUTS ON FURLOUGH, 1942. On leave from the Royal Canadian Air Force, Bobby Bauer, Mrs. Bauer, and Woody Dumart take in a Braves-Reds game at Braves Field. When the war broke out, the Kraut Line (Bauer, Dumart, and Milt Schmidt) joined the Royal Canadian Air Force together. (Collection of the Sports Museum.)

BEP GUIDOLIN. In November 1942, Bep Guidolin became the youngest player in NHL history at the age of 16 years 11 months. Because of the talent shortage caused by World War II, a lot of young players, old players, and minor-leaguers got to play in the big time. Guidolin played for the Bruins until 1947, before being traded to Chicago, but returned to coach the team from 1973 to 1974. (Courtesy of J. Harvey McKenney.)

THE BRUINS IN ACTION AGAINST THE BLACKHAWKS, 1942. Frank Brimsek watches the puck skitter away from the Hawks Red Hamill in front of the net as Busher Jackson (18), Des Smith (8), and

Roy Conacher (9) move in. (Collection of the Sports Museum.)

FRANK BRIMSEK RECEIVES HIS DISCHARGE FROM THE COAST GUARD, 1945. One of the few Americans in the NHL, Frank Brimsek served in the U.S. Coast Guard during World War II. (Collection of the Sports Museum, U.S. Coast Guard photograph.)

A Frank Brimsek Bruins Program, 1946. Frank Brimsek had the unenviable task of replacing the popular Tiny Thompson. He more than fulfilled fan expectations, registering six shutouts in his first eight games while forging a Hockey Hall of Fame career. (Collection of the Sports Museum.)

ART ROSS AND PAT EGAN. Pat Egan, also known as "the Flying Boxcar," played 294 games for the Bruins between 1943 and 1949, made an appearance in the 1949 NHL All-Star Game, and won the Dufresne Trophy (outstanding Bruin in home games) that same year. He had the distinction of wearing jersey No. 2, made famous by Eddie Shore, and later retired. (Collection of the Sports Museum, photograph by Leslie Jones.)

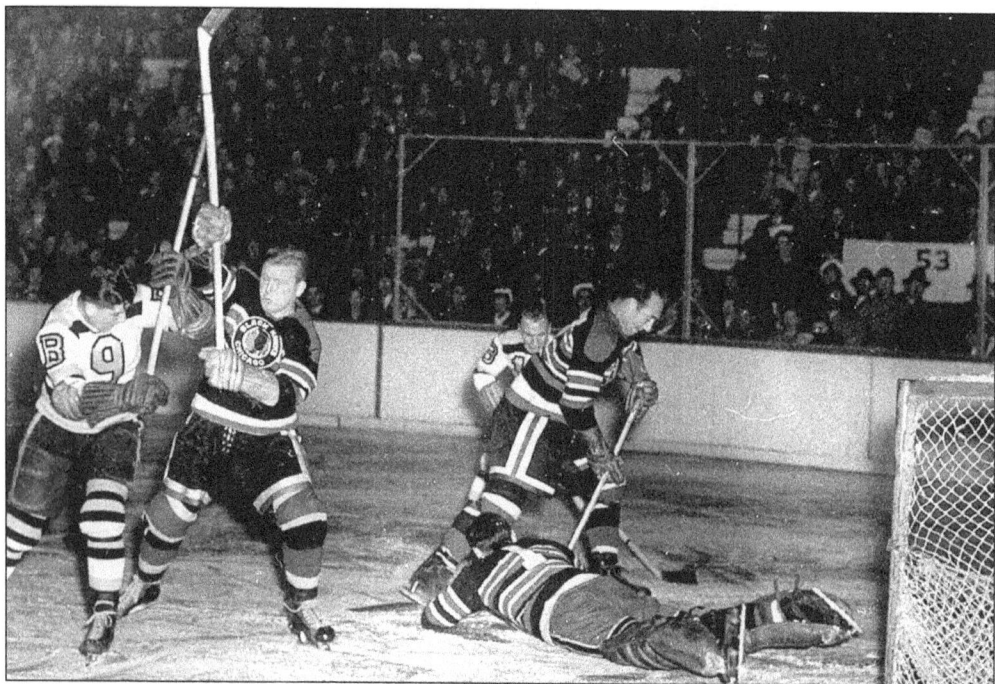

BRUINS ON THE ATTACK, 1944. Bruins center Frankie Mario attempts to score on Mike Karakas of Chicago in the 1944 season opener. Karakas, like Frank Brimsek, was a Minnesota native. The Bruins went on to win 7-5. (Collection of the Sports Museum.)

DIT CLAPPER. The ever dapper Dit Clapper moved behind the bench after 20 years in black and gold. He coached the team from 1945 to 1949. (Collection of the Sports Museum.)

GENE MACK'S VIEW OF BRUINS HISTORY, 1946. As a sports cartoonist, Gene Mack had the rare ability to tell the story of the game in a single panel. This cartoon takes it a step further,

telling the entire history of the team at the Boston Garden from 1928 to 1946. (Collection of the Sports Museum.)

Young Bruin Hopefuls at the Boston Arena, 1949. From left to right are Buck Boucher, Milt Schmidt, Jack McIntyre, Gordie Byers, Norm Corcoran, Obie O'Brien, and an unidentified

player at Bruins training camp in the Boston Arena. (Collection of the Sports Museum.)

MOE HENDERSON AND FERNIE FLAMAN, 1949. Moe Henderson played eight seasons in the NHL, all with Boston. Signed by the Bruins towards the end of World War II, the six-foot-tall, 180-pound defenseman brought some size to the Bruins blue line in the late 1940s and early 1950s. After single-game stints with the Bruins in the 1946 and 1947 seasons, Fernie Flaman made the team for good in 1948 and became a regular the following season. Partnering with such defensive stalwarts as Pat Egan, Johnny Crawford, and Bill Quackenbush, Flaman established himself as a force in front of the net. (Collection of the Sports Museum.)

THE BRUINS TEE OFF, 1949. Shown from left to right, Woody Dumart, Pat Egan, and Milt Schmidt used a different kind of stick when the trio played golf at the Commonwealth Country Club. (Collection of the Sports Museum.)

JIM PETERS, MILT SCHMIDT, AND WOODY DUMART, 1949. Captain Milt Schmidt is flanked by Jim Peters (left) and longtime linemate Woody Dumart. The "24-49" on the jersey crest is a reference to the Bruins 25th anniversary. It was the first sweater to feature the spoked "B" logo. (Collection of the Sports Museum.)

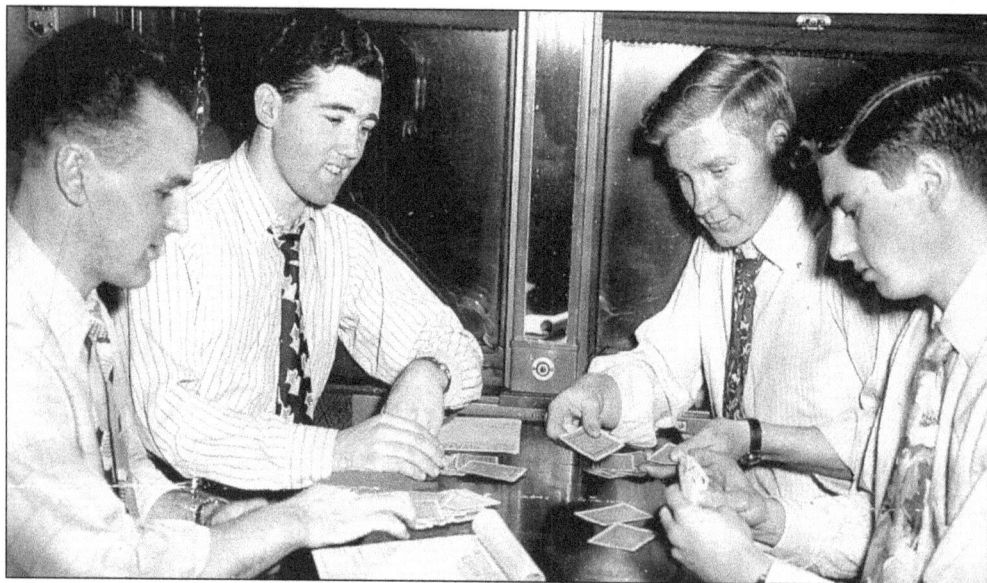

PASSING TIME ON A TRAIN RIDE, 1948. In the days before plane travel, teams made road trips by rail. Card games were a popular way to pass the time. On a trip to Toronto, Paul Ronty, center of the "Muscle Line," deals while Johnny Pierson smiles and Ed Harrison studies his hand. Pete Babando is on the far left. (Collection of the Sports Museum.)

Four

THE 1950s

BRUINS RECEIVING AWARDS, 1950. Clarence Campbell, NHL president, presents the C.F. Adams Memorial Trophy to captain Milt Schmidt and the Calder Trophy to Jack Gelineau. Named after Frank Calder, the first president of the NHL, the Calder Trophy is presented to the rookie of the year. (Collection of the Sports Museum.)

FERNIE FLAMAN AND HIS SON TERRY. In later years, Terry Flaman led both Thayer Academy and Harvard as hockey captain and was an inspiration to all who knew him. Stricken with cancer while only in his 30s, Terry was present at many of the games his father coached at Northeastern University. His speech between periods, delivered in a wheelchair, helped inspire the Huskies to their Beanpot triumph on February 13, 1984. He passed away two months later at age 37. (Photograph by Al Ruelle.)

JOHN PEIRSON. John Peirson checks out a new pair of skates while awaiting treatment for a thigh injury. People today remember Peirson as the excellent hockey analyst on WSBK TV38, but he was also quite a hockey player. In his time with the Bruins, he averaged more than 20 goals a season in a six-season stretch between 1948 and 1954. He was once described as a player who had "more scoring opportunities than a good pitcher has deliveries." Peirson finished his career with more than 150 goals. (Collection of the Sports Museum, photograph by Leslie Jones.)

ED SANDFORD. After Ed Sandford captained and sparked St. Michael's College (a high school in Toronto) to the 1947 Memorial Cup, he was quickly signed by Art Ross, the vice president and general manager. "Sandy" joined the club in 1947 along with his cousin Ed Harrison, and they were dubbed the "Gold Dust Twins" by Bruin defenseman John Crawford. Though injuries slowed his career, Sandford was a fine two-way player who scored more than 100 goals in his nine-year career. Sandford has served for many years as a goal judge at Bruins games. (Collection of the Sports Museum, photograph by Al Ruelle.)

PAUL RONTY. Ranger goalie Chuck Rayner plays the puck off his stick while Paul Ronty sweeps behind the net. A product of the Bruins system, Ronty played for Boston from 1947 to 1951 and was a member of the Muscle Line with Kenny Smith and Johnny Peirson. He also played for the Boston Olympics during the 1945–1946 season. Note the harsh shadows caused by the early television lights. (Collection of the Sports Museum.)

THE FIGHTING LEADERS OF THE BRUINS, 1950. Coach Lynn Patrick emphasizes a point to captain Milt Schmidt and alternate captains Bill Quackenbush and Eddie Sandford. (Collection

of the Sports Museum.)

BACHELOR BRUINS, 1950. Some eligible young Bruin bachelors put on the Ritz with their dates at the annual team family party. From left to right are Jack Gelineau and Virginia Lawrence, Bill Quackenbush and Joan Kalloch, Dave Creighton and Lucia Libbey, and Johnny Peirson and Bunny Hoagland. (Collection of the Sports Museum, photograph by Leslie Jones.)

VETERAN LINEMATES, 1953. Veterans Joe Klukay (left), Milt Schmidt (center), and Cal Gardner face off against the Canadiens in the 1953 season opener. (Collection of the Sports Museum.)

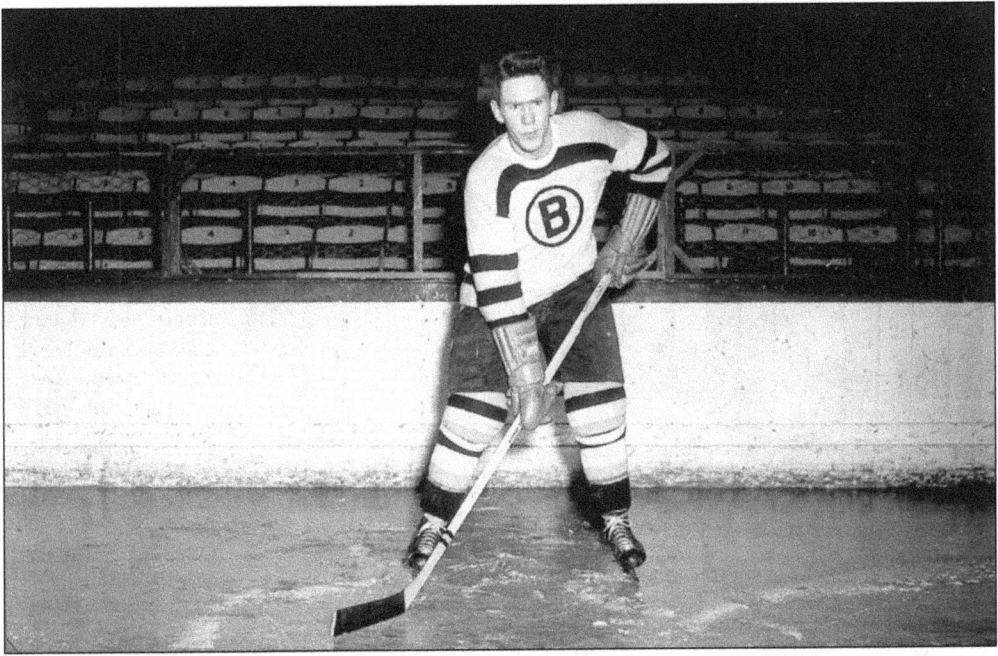

LEO LABINE. The body checker was a big crowd favorite with his tenacious style of play. Known as the "Haileybury Hurricane," LaBine's job was to shadow and hound the opposing team's scoring stars. He was a scrapper who was very skilled with his fists as well as his tongue. His confrontations with the great Maurice "Rocket" Richard are legendary. In 1958, NHL general managers named him in their top five list of the toughest players in the league. The colorful LaBine chipped in offensively as well, scoring 123 goals during his Bruins career. (Collection of the Sports Museum, photograph by Al Ruelle.)

BRUINS TEE OFF AT THE CHARLES RIVER COUNTRY CLUB. From left to right are Woody Dumart, Milt Schmidt, Lynn Patrick, Bill Quackenbush, and Johnny Peirson. (Collection of the Sports Museum.)

JOHNNY PEIRSON AND HAMMY MOORE. Trainer Hammy Moore shows Johnny Peirson a protective mask that he designed. Peirson, who had been out of action for three weeks due to a compound jaw fracture, would return to the ice wearing the mask. Moore had made similar face guards for Bill Cowley and Milt Schmidt. (Collection of the Sports Museum.)

BRUINS PLAYERS WITH TOMMY COLLINS, 1953. Bruins players visit boxer Tommy Collins before his fight with Fabela Chavez at the Boston Arena. From left to right are Milt Schmidt, Red Sullivan, Collins, Warren Godfrey, and Jerry Toppazzini. Note that Sullivan and Toppazzini are wearing Hershey Bears jackets. The Bears were a longtime Bruins farm club. (Collection of the Sports Museum.)

THE HANDSHAKE. Perhaps the most famous hockey photograph of all time, it is certainly one of the most poignant. On the night of April 8, 1952, the Bruins played Montreal at the Forum in the seventh game of a hard-fought semifinal series. Habs star Maurice "Rocket" Richard collided with Leo Labine and then crashed into the knee of Bill Quackenbush. Stunned and bleeding, he was taken from the ice. Despite six stitches in his head, Richard returned to the bench groggy and disoriented. With four minutes to go and the score tied at 1-1, Montreal coach Dick Irvin let the Rocket back onto the ice. Seconds later, he made an electrifying rush through the Bruins defense and slipped the puck past goalie Sugar Jim Henry. The Forum erupted as the Canadiens won the game and the series. This picture shows Henry, eyes blackened and nose broken from an injury earlier in the series, congratulating Richard after the game. He bows slightly as Richard, blood dripping from the bandage on his forehead, shakes his hand. Back in the dressing room, Richard, overcome with emotion, broke down and sobbed uncontrollably. The hero of the series had played on instinct, heart, and desire, not even remembering the goal he scored. (Courtesy of the John Brooks Collection.)

BILL QUACKENBUSH. In 1949, Bill Quackenbush became the first defenseman in NHL history to win the Lady Byng Trophy. He skated seven seasons with Boston and tutored many young upcoming Bruin defensemen in their craft. He was elected to the Hockey Hall of Fame in 1978. (Collection of the Sports Museum.)

FLEMING MACKELL. "Flaming" Fleming, with his spectacular buzz-saw skating style, was a fan favorite ever since his arrival in Boston in 1952. Mackell captured the Dufresne Trophy (outstanding Bruin in home games) and first team all-star honors in his first full season in the black and gold. Mackell was also a proven clutch performer as he led all scorers in the 1958 playoffs. (Collection of the Sports Museum, photograph by Al Ruelle.)

MILT SCHMIDT. Schmidt is the only player to have his name inscribed on the Stanley Cup as a Bruin four times. He won two Stanley Cups as a player, in 1939 and 1941, and he won another two as general manager, in 1970 and 1972. NHL president Clarence Campbell once remarked that, "Milt Schmidt played so hard and was so tough that he left a little bit of himself on the ice in every game he played." Schmidt was elected to the Hockey Hall of Fame in 1961, and his No. 15 was retired by the Bruins. (Collection of the Sports Museum.)

FERNIE FLAMAN KNOCKS MAURICE RICHARD INTO THE NET, 1955. When it came to defending the territory in front of the net, Fernie Flaman gave no quarter. Flaman fought battles with some of the premier hard hitters of the era: Rocket Richard, Ted Lindsay, and Lou Fontinato.

He never backed down from a fight. He led the NHL in penalties in 1955 but was also a second team all-star that season, as well as in 1957 and 1958. (Collection of the Sports Museum, photograph by David Bier.)

REAL CHEVREFILS. A product of Timmons, Ontario (the hometown of Frank and Peter Mahovlich), Chevrefils was traded to Detroit as a part of the deal that brought Terry Sawchuck to Boston. He came back within a year in another multiplayer deal. After leaving Boston for good in 1959, he played in the minors until 1964. This was not unusual; with only six NHL clubs there were not enough jobs for all the talent available. The level of play in the American Hockey League (AHL), Western Hockey League (WHL), and Central Hockey League (CHL) was quite high, and many players spent their whole careers in the minors. (Collection of the Sports Museum.)

DON MCKENNEY. Don McKenney came up through the Bruins system, playing junior hockey with the Barrie Flyers of the Ontario Hockey Association and spending a year with the Hershey Bears of the AHL before arriving in Boston in the 1954–1955 season. A frequent top-ten scorer, he helped the Bruins reach the Stanley Cup finals in both 1957 and 1958 and won the Lady Byng Trophy in the 1959–1960 season. McKenney captained the Bruins from 1961 to 1963 before he was traded to the Rangers in February of that year. (Collection of the Sports Museum.)

COACH MILT SCHMIDT. Milt Schmidt hugs goalie Don Simmons following Boston's stunning upset victory over the Detroit Red Wings in the 1957 Stanley Cup semifinals. Boston captured the best of seven series by a score of four games to one. (Courtesy of J. Harvey McKenney.)

HAL LAYCOE. Laycoe was a rarity in that he wore glasses on the ice. He is best remembered for his part in what became known as the "Richard Riot." On March 13, 1955, he got into a stick-swinging duel with Montreal's fiery star Maurice Richard. Richard broke a stick over Laycoe, and when linesman Cliff Thompson tried to break it up, Richard attacked him, too. NHL president Clarence Campbell suspended Richard for the rest of the season, including the playoffs. Montreal was outraged with Campbell. On March 17, the Canadiens played their next game against Detroit, with whom they were tied for first place. Despite threats against him, Campbell attended the game (the NHL had its headquarters in Montreal at the time). As the score climbed to 4-0 in Detroit's favor, more and more abuse was directed towards Campbell, including a punch thrown by a fan. Then, during the first intermission, a smoke bomb went off, forcing the evacuation of the Forum. The crowd rampaged down St. Catherine Street, smashing windows, looting stores, and overturning cars. The next day, from the ravaged Forum, Richard spoke on the radio and called for an end to the rioting. The Canadiens finished behind Detroit and eventually lost to the Red Wings in the finals. (Collection of the Sports Museum.)

DON CHERRY. Cherry's professional hockey career spanned 20 years, but he only played one game in the NHL. Wearing No. 24, he took to the ice on March 31, 1955, against Montreal at the Forum. Cherry did not figure in the scoring and returned to the Hershey Bears. After he retired as a player, he turned to coaching, then broadcasting. Today, he is one of the most popular and recognized commentators in the game. (Collection of the Sports Museum.)

TERRY SAWCHUCK. Sawchuck was one of the greatest goaltenders of all time. Brooding, sensitive, and nervous, he played most of his career for the Detroit Red Wings. Traded to the Bruins in a multiplayer deal in 1955, he was never happy in Boston. He was traded back to Detroit in 1957 for John Bucyk, a future Bruins captain and Hall of Famer. Claimed by Toronto in the 1964 intra-league draft, he teamed up with another "old man," Johnny Bower, and helped the Maple Leafs win the last Stanley Cup of the preexpansion era (1967). (Collection of the Sports Museum.)

Sport News BOSTON BRUINS HOCKEY

JOHN BUCYK

OFFICIAL PROGRAM 25¢

Boston Garden

JOHN BUCYK. Bucyk came to the Bruins in the trade that sent Terry Sawchuck back to Detroit. He joined former teammate Vic Stasiuk and, later, Bronco Horvath to form the "Uke Line." They played together until 1961. "The Chief" went on to play for the Bruins until 1978, a total of 21 seasons. (Collection of the Sports Museum, photograph by Al Ruelle.)

THE UKE LINE. Herb Ralby coined the name Uke (for Ukrainian) Line, although only Stasiuk and Bucyk were of Ukrainian descent. Pictured from left to right, Vic Stasiuk, Bronco Horvath, and Johnny Bucyk played together on the Edmonton Flyers before coming to the NHL. (Collection of the Sports Museum.)

VIC STASIUK. Right winger Vic Stasiuk scored 125 goals for the Bruins in his five seasons. He scored most of those goals on the famed Uke Line with partners Bronco Horvath and Johnny Bucyk. (Collection of the Sports Museum, photograph by Al Ruelle.)

BRONCO HORVATH. Horvath arrived in Boston in 1957 and was quickly reunited with his old linemates, Vic Stasiuk and John Bucyk, from Edmonton of the Western Hockey League. Horvath played center on the Uke Line, and in the 1959–1960 season, he led the NHL with 39 goals, missing the scoring title by one point. Using his incredible slap shot, he went on to pot 103 goals for the Bruins. (Collection of the Sports Museum, photograph by Al Ruelle.)

WILLIE O'REE AND FLEMING MACKELL. O'Ree and Mackell talk prior to O'Ree's historic NHL debut at the Montreal Forum on January 18, 1958. Although his career consisted of only 45 games, he will always be remembered as the first black player in the NHL. He spent most of his career in the minors before retiring in 1980. (Boston Herald photograph.)

FERNIE FLAMAN. Fernie Flaman spent 17 years in the NHL, mostly with the Bruins. A top stay-at-home defenseman, he jealously guarded the area in front of his net. Flaman came up with the Bruins in 1948 and became a regular the following season. He was traded to Toronto in 1950 (where he helped the Leafs win a Stanley Cup) but was traded back in 1955, along with his defense partner Leo Boivin, another ferocious body checker. Fern Flaman played seven more seasons with the Bruins before moving to the AHL as a player-coach with the Providence Reds. (Collection of the Sports Museum.)

THE 1957 STANLEY CUP PLAYOFFS. The Bruins played some memorable playoffs against the Habs in the 1950s. They could not derail the Montreal juggernaut, however. The Canadiens won five consecutive Stanley Cups, from 1956 to 1960, still an NHL record. (Collection of the Sports Museum.)

Five

1960–1966

FERNIE FLAMAN NIGHT. A bemused Fernie Flaman sits amid the gifts bestowed upon him on Fernie Flaman Night at the Boston Garden on December 30, 1960. The popular Flaman served as the Bruins captain from 1955 to 1961. (Collection of the Sports Museum.)

LEO BOIVIN. Only five feet eight inches tall, Leo Boivin was one of the fiercest body checkers in NHL history. Originally a Bruins prospect, the Prescott, Ontario, native was traded to Toronto, where he was first teamed up with Fernie Flaman, another hard-hitting defenseman. Flaman and Boivin were traded to back to Boston in the 1955–1956 season, and Boivin remained with the Bruins for 11 years, wearing the captain's "C" from 1963 to 1966. Tim Horton, perhaps the strongest player of his era, called Boivin the toughest defenseman in the league to get by, and many players rated him the hardest hitter in the league. (Collection of the Sports Museum.)

THE BRUINS IN ACTION AGAINST MONTREAL, 1960. Don Simmons, wearing an early face mask, has the unenviable task of trying to keep Jean Beliveau from scoring as Autrey Erickson and Fernie Flaman move in to help. Simmons made the save, but the Bruins went on to lose to the Habs 5-1. (Boston Herald photograph.)

BRONCO HORVATH RECEIVES THE DUFRESNE TROPHY, 1960. Bronco Horvath is honored in a pregame ceremony for being voted the most valuable Bruins player in home games. Bob Salmon, a United Press International sports reporter, presents Horvath with the Elizabeth C. Dufresne Trophy to the cheers of 13,675 fans. The versatile trophy doubled as an ashtray. (Boston Herald photograph.)

HARRY LUMLEY. The quintessential journeyman, Lumley had a long NHL career in the 1940s and 1950s. Along the way, he picked up a Vezina Trophy (1954) and played on three all-star teams (1951, 1954, and 1955). Boston was his last NHL stop, where he played 78 games over three seasons. (Boston Herald photograph.)

DON SIMMONS. In the days of the six-team league, goalies like Don Simmons were fated to spend most of their time on the bench or in the minors. Simmons played in 247 games over 11 NHL seasons with Boston, Toronto, and New York and even played in the 1963 NHL All-Star Game. After his playing days were over, he went into the goaltending equipment business. (Boston Herald photograph.)

COACH PHIL WATSON. Phil Watson had been a star with the Rangers in the 1930s and 1940s. He became the Rangers coach in 1955, but his tough, abrasive (some said abusive) style alienated many players. Once, when the Blueshirts lost to the Canadiens 5-1 in what he perceived to be a lackluster performance, Watson made them return to the ice after the game for a grueling practice session. Wearing out his welcome in New York, the fiery coach came to Boston in 1961. It was a challenging task, as he was replacing Milt Schmidt and taking over a last-place team. His tenure lasted until 1963, when Schmidt returned to the bench. (Boston Herald photograph.)

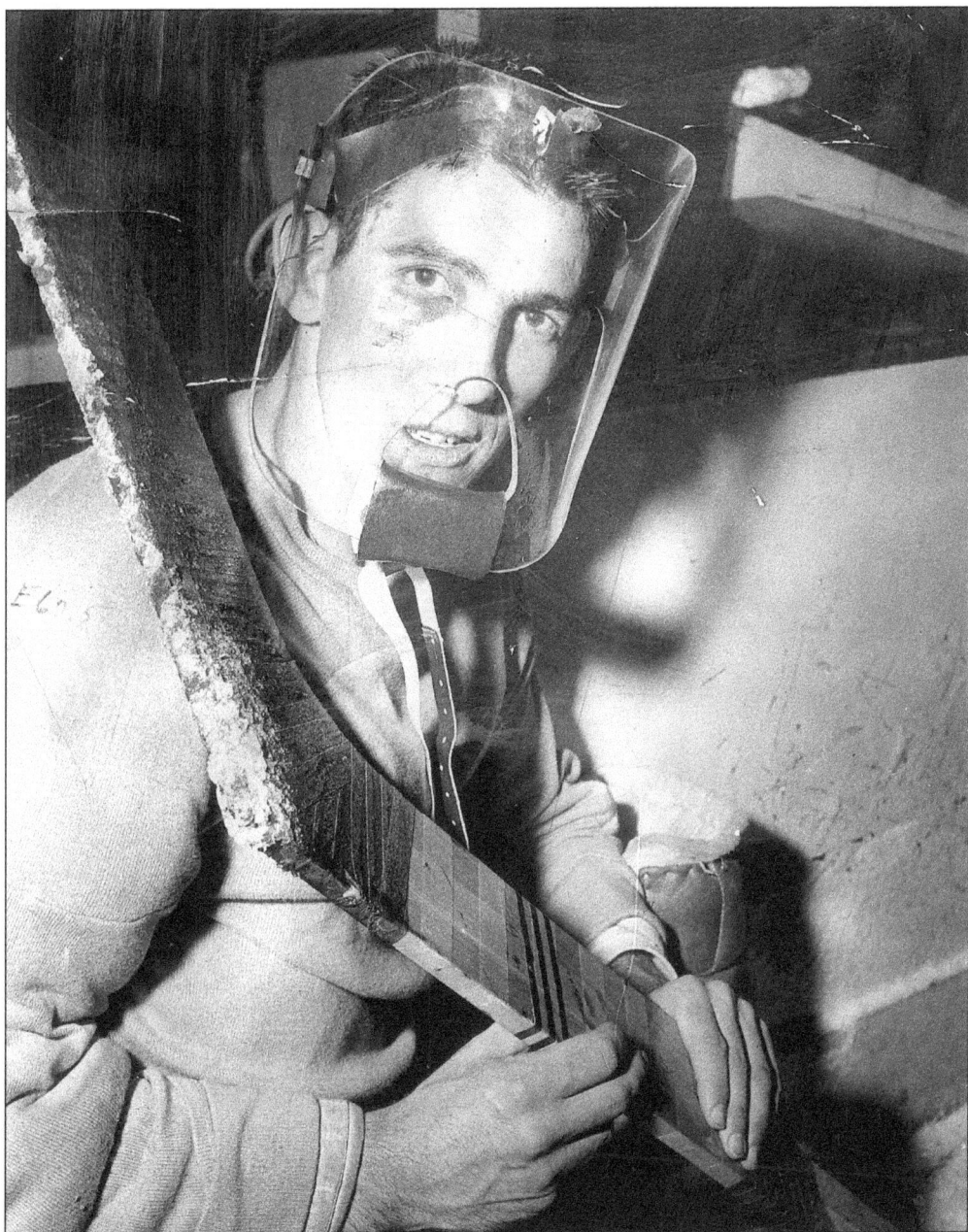

DON SIMMONS WITH AN EXPERIMENTAL MASK, 1959. Although Jacques Plante introduced the goalie mask in November 1959, they were still a novelty. When Bruin goaltender Don Simmons was injured in December, he donned this unusual plastic shield. Masks for goaltenders did not become commonplace until the mid-1960s, with Andy Brown of Detroit going barefaced as late as 1973. (Boston Herald photograph.)

PROTECTION MEETING, 1960. Charles Prescott (left) of Bennett, Inc. points to a protective clip on the back of a skate blade held by Lynn Patrick, Bruins general manager, as compared to an old sharp pointed blade, as Bronco Horvath looks on. The clip was an experiment in the search to prevent injuries to players caused by the sharp skate blade heels. The clip was never widely adapted, but plastic caps were put on all skate blades until a total redesign in the 1980s (still in use today) eliminated the problem. (Boston Herald photograph.)

DON HEAD AND PAT STAPLETON, 1961. The two rookies are probably thinking, "What have we gotten ourselves into?" Head played one dismal season in Boston before returning to the WHL. Defenseman Pat Stapleton played only two seasons for the Bruins before eventually becoming a star in Chicago. (Boston Herald photograph.)

PAT STAPLETON, 1961. Although he played on some losing teams in Boston, Pat Stapleton was a standout defenseman. Traded to Toronto with Orland Kurtenbach and Andy Hebenton for Ron Stewart in 1965, he was claimed by Chicago in the intra-league draft the next day. With the Blackhawks, he was an all-star in 1967, 1969, 1971, and 1972 before jumping to the Chicago Cougars of the World Hockey Association (WHA).

JERRY TOPPAZZINI. "Topper" began his career with the Bruins before he was traded to Chicago in 1954. He returned to the Bruins by way of Detroit in 1956, where he played until 1964. A three-time all-star (1955, 1958, and 1959), Toppazzini played on some of the best and worst Bruins teams. (Boston Herald photograph.)

DON HEAD. Don Head began his professional career with the Portland Buckaroos of the WHL before being traded to the Bruins in 1961. In his one major-league season (1961–1962), he shared the net with Bruce Gamble (Ed Chadwick played four games) and won 9 games, lost 26, and tied 3. The following year, he returned to the west coast and played the rest of his 11-year professional career in the WHL with Portland and Seattle. (Boston Herald photograph.)

TOMMY WILLIAMS.
Minnesota native Williams was, at the time, the only American-born player in the NHL. "The Bomber" was a steady performer who also saw duty with Minnesota, California, and Washington, as well as in the WHA. (Boston Herald photograph.)

WAYNE CONNELLY AND TOMMY WILLIAMS, 1962. Prominent players in the Bruins youth movement, Connelly and Williams were expected to help the hapless Bruins out of the NHL cellar. That was not the case. Connelly played only briefly in Boston, and Williams played eight seasons for mostly losing Bruins clubs. (Boston Herald photograph.)

ORLAND KURTENBACH, 1961. Claimed by the Bruins on waivers from New York, the six-foot-two-inch Kurtenbach added some size and muscle to the Bruins lineup. He also played for the Maple Leafs and Rangers before going to Vancouver in the 1970 expansion draft (Bruin defenseman Gary Doak was also claimed by the Canucks). Kurtenbach became Vancouver's first captain and one of its most popular stars. (Boston Herald photograph.)

DOUG MOHNS. A Bruin from 1953 to 1964, Mohns played in seven NHL All-Star Games over an NHL career that lasted 22 seasons. "Diesel" won the Dufresne Trophy in 1962. (Boston Herald photograph.)

PHIL WATSON AND LEO MONAHAN.
Phil Watson discusses the game with
Boston Record American hockey
writer D. Leo Monahan during
a practice session at the Garden.
(Boston Herald photograph.)

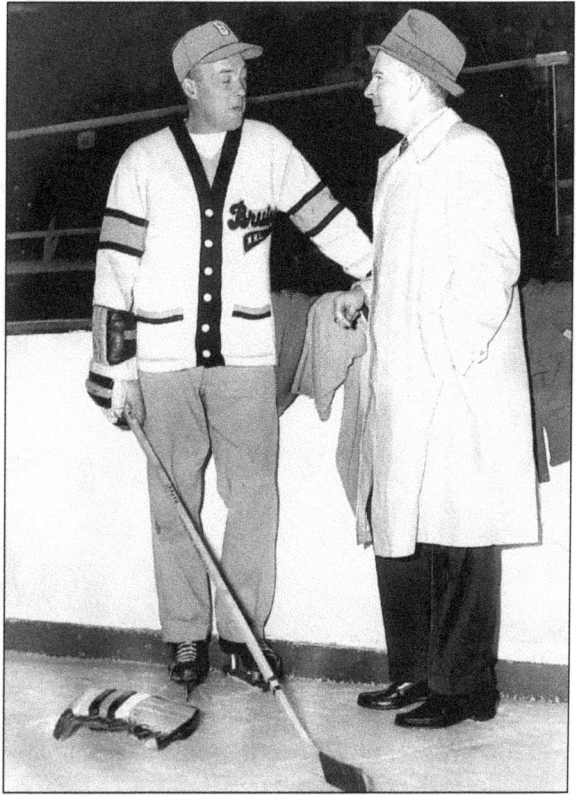

BRUCE GAMBLE. In the days when the
starting goalie played most games,
the backup was usually a journeyman
who was no stranger to the minors.
Expansion created opportunities for
goaltenders who previously could
not hope to crack the six-team NHL.
Gamble played two seasons in Boston,
backing up Eddie Johnston, before
moving on to Toronto. (Boston
Herald photograph.)

113

A BRUIN MEETS A BRUIN, 1963. Bruins rookie Don Awrey meets a Russian bruin, a trained bear from the Moscow Circus. The circus was a popular attraction at the Garden and was always good for a photograph opportunity. Shown with Awrey are Bruins president Walter Brown (left) and bear trainer Valentin Filatov. (Boston Herald photograph.)

JACK STEWART AND TED GREEN, 1964. Defense stars of the past and present meet at the Garden. "Black Jack" Stewart, an all-star defenseman and Hall of Famer, chats with Bruins star defenseman Ted Green. Stewart was in Boston as the presiding judge for the harness meeting at Suffolk Downs racetrack. (Boston Herald photograph.)

WESTON ADAMS AS A GOALIE AT PHILLIPS EXETER ACADEMY,
1923. The future Bruins president would also play freshman
hockey at Harvard. (Boston Herald photograph.)

WESTON ADAMS. Weston Adams succeeded
Walter Brown as president of the Bruins after
Brown's death in 1964. He served as president
until 1969, when his son, Weston Jr., took
over. Adams oversaw the club in the transition
period between the Original Six and the
12-team league. During his tenure, the Bruins
went from cellar dwellers to Stanley Cup
contenders, thanks in no small part to the
arrival of such stars as Bobby Orr, Phil Esposito,
Derek Sanderson, and Gerry Cheevers. (Boston
Herald photograph.)

COACH MILT SCHMIDT WITH REGGIE FLEMING AND AB MCDONALD, 1965. After a stellar career with the Bruins, Milt Schmidt moved behind the bench (1954–1961 and 1962–1966) and, later, into the front office (1967–1972). Here, he dispenses advice to Reg Fleming (left) and Ab McDonald (right). Both players came to Boston from Chicago in a trade for longtime star Doug Mohns. While the white uniform worn by Fleming remained (with minor changes) a Bruin standard from the 1950s to the late 1960s, McDonald's black jersey was one of the many dark sweater variations worn by the Bruins in that period. (Boston Herald photograph.)

REG FLEMING, 1965. Bruin Reg Fleming tries on the fur hat of Victor Kuzkin. Kuzkin was a member of the world champion Russian amateur team, which had just arrived in Toronto for a hockey tour of Canada. Amateurs in name only, the Soviet squads of this era featured the top talent in the Eastern Bloc. With the collapse of the Soviet Union, the best players were finally free to play professionally. (Boston Herald photograph.)

FORBES KENNEDY AND HIS BROTHER JAKE, 1965. Forbes Kennedy, recuperating from a shoulder separation, skates at the Boston Garden to keep in shape. With him is his brother Jake, a promising player who lost a leg from the knee down in a hockey mishap at age 16. (Boston Herald photograph.)

BRUINS GOALTENDERS AT THE 1965 TRAINING CAMP. In the preexpansion era, competition for goaltending spots was tough. Two youngsters hoping to make the big club, Bernie Parent (left) and Gerry Cheevers (right), chat with veteran goaltender Eddie Johnston (center). Cheevers and Johnston went on to backbone the Bruins through the Stanley Cup years (1970 and 1972), while Parent is remembered as the one who got away, claimed by Philadelphia in the 1967 expansion draft. Both Parent and Cheevers were eventually elected to the Hockey Hall of Fame. (Boston Herald photograph.)

EDDIE WESTFALL. After coming up to
the Bruins in the 1961–1962 season,
Westfall established himself as a
defensive forward and quiet leader.
After playing on two Stanley Cup
teams with the Bruins, he was claimed
by the New York Islanders in the 1972
expansion draft. He went on to be one
of the most popular players in Islanders
history. (Boston Herald photograph.)

EDDIE WESTFALL. Eddie Westfall gags it up
with Bruno Fuseo, costumed for his part as
a gladiator in an upcoming Italian festival.
Westfall was one of the players who were
with the Bruins through both the lean years
and glory years, along with Ed Johnston,
John Bucyk, Ted Green, and Dallas Smith.
(Boston Herald photograph.)

119

THE B'NAI B'RITH AWARDS CEREMONY, 1964. Some of the finest athletes of their generation are honored by the B'nai B'rith. From left to right are Eddie Shore, Jessie Owen, Sen. Ted Kennedy, Sandy Koufax, NHL president Clarence Campbell, and Paavo Nurmi. (Boston Herald photograph.)

EDDIE JOHNSTON. "EJ," shown battling the Canadiens' Dick Duff, is the last man in NHL history to play every minute in goal for his team throughout an entire season, playing 4,200 minutes over 70 games for the last-place Bruins in the 1962–1963 season. After playing on some of the worst teams in NHL history, things improved for the long-suffering goalie in the late 1960s. With the arrival of Bobby Orr, Phil Esposito, and Gerry Cheevers (among others), the Bruins became an NHL powerhouse, winning Stanley Cups in 1970 and 1972. After the 1972–1973 season, Johnston was sent to the Maple Leafs to complete the deal that brought Jacques Plante to Boston. (Boston Herald photograph.)

THE PICTURE TELLS THE STORY. The clock shows a 5-2 Rangers lead as goalie Ed Johnston leans dejectedly on the net. Although the Bruins of the early 1960s lost a lot of games, the picture shows that they still packed them in. Bruins attendance at the Garden consistently exceeded that of the Celtics, who were, at the time, the best team in basketball. (Boston Herald photograph.)

DALLAS SMITH, 1960. After a five-game tryout in the 1959–1960 season, Smith played all 70 games for the Bruins in the 1960–1961 season. Although he would not be back again as a regular until 1967, he went on to play 10 solid seasons in black and gold. (Boston Herald photograph.)

HARRY SINDEN. Sinden was considered one of the greatest amateur defensemen in Canadian history. He captained the Whitby Dunlops and led the Canadian Olympic team to a silver medal in the 1960 Olympics in Squaw Valley. He attended several Bruins training camps as a player prior to being named head coach in 1966. (Photograph by Al Ruelle.)

TED GREEN. Ted Green had the well-deserved nickname "Terrible Ted." Green was the Bruins enforcer throughout his entire NHL career, from 1961 to 1972, during which he fought every heavyweight the league had to offer. Not just a fighter, Green played in the 1965 and 1969 All-Star Games. (Collection of the Sports Museum.)

FULL HOUSE BUT NO CIGAR, 1966. Ron Murphy beats Montreal defenseman J.C. Tremblay and goalie Gump Worsley but misses the net. The Bruins in the early 1960s usually played to

full houses at the Garden despite their losing records and, as this picture demonstrates, bad luck. (Boston Herald photograph.)

GILLES MAROTTE. A talented defenseman, Marotte is best known as a key player in perhaps the greatest trade in Bruins history. On May 15, 1967, Marotte, along with Pit Matin and Jack Norris, were dealt to Chicago for Phil Esposito, Ken Hodge, and Fred Stanfield. While Martin had a long, productive career with the Blackhawks, Marotte played only three seasons in Chicago, and Jack Norris, a minor-league goalie, played a total of 58 NHL games; 10 with the Blackhawks. None were ever the stars that Esposito, Hodge, and Stanfield became for Boston. (Boston Herald photograph.)

126

THE PLAYER OF THE FUTURE. Even as a teenager, Bobby Orr was heralded as a phenomenon. Signed to play junior hockey in Oshawa when he was only 14, Orr is shown with Weston Adams at a Generals game in 1964. In 1966, at the age of 18, Orr signed a record-breaking contract to play for the Bruins, and the rest is history. (Boston Herald photograph.)

Signing Bobby Orr. The Bruins and indeed the game of hockey moved into a new era with the signing of Bobby Orr to his first professional contract. Meeting with general manager Leighton "Hap" Emms (left) aboard Emms's cruiser, the *Barbara Lynn*, the 18-year-old Orr, accompanied by his father, Doug, inks a deal to suit up for the black and gold. (Boston Herald photograph.)

Visit us at
arcadiapublishing.com

www.ingramcontent.com/pod-product-compliance
Lightning Source LLC
Chambersburg PA
CBHW080603110426
42813CB00006B/1393